BTEC
Level 2

advancing learning, changing lives

CREATIVE MEDIA PRODUCTION | LEVEL 2

BTEC First

Paul Baylis | Natalie Procter

Published by Pearson Education Limited, a company incorporated in England and Wales, having its registered office at Edinburgh Gate, Harlow, Essex, CM20 2JE. Registered company number: 872828

www.pearsonschoolsandfecolleges.co.uk

Edexcel is a registered trademark of Edexcel Limited

Text © Pearson Education Limited 2010

First published 2010

13 12 11 10
10 9 8 7 6 5 4 3 2 1

British Library Cataloguing in Publication Data

A catalogue record for this book is available from the British Library.

ISBN 978 1 846906 73 2

Edited by David Mantovani
Designed by Wooden Ark
Typeset by Phoenix Photosetting
Original illustrations © Pearson 2010
Illustrated by Vicky Woodgate
Cover design by Visual Philosophy, created by eMC Design
Picture research by Emma Whyte
Front cover photo © ImageSource
Back cover photos © Shutterstock/Stanislav Komogorov and Shutterstock/Miodrag Gajic
Printed in Italy

Disclaimer

This material has been published on behalf of Edexcel and offers high-quality support for the delivery of Edexcel qualifications. This does not mean that the material is essential to achieve any Edexcel qualification, nor does it mean that it is the only suitable material available to support any Edexcel qualification. Edexcel material will not be used verbatim in setting any Edexcel examination or assessment. Any resource lists produced by Edexcel shall include this and other appropriate resources.

Copies of official specifications for all Edexcel qualifications may be found on the Edexcel website: www.edexcel.com

Hotlinks

There are links to relevant websites in this book. In order to ensure that the links are up to date, that the links works, and that the sites are not inadvertently linked to sites that could be considered offensive, we have made the links available on the following website: www.pearsonhotlinks.co.uk. When you access the site, type in the title of the book or the ISBN to access the page containing the links for this book.

Contents

Mandatory units

Unit	Credit value	Title	Page
1	5	Research for creative media production	1
2	5	Communication techniques for creative media production	27
3	5	The creative media sector	53
4	5	Media audiences and products	77

Process chapters

Title	Page
Investigation	105
Pre-production	121
Production	141
Post-production	171
Review	191

Assessment and grading criteria grids for optional units	211
Fact files	220
Glossary	224
Index	227

About the authors

Paul Baylis is Director of Curriculum at North Nottinghamshire College. He has over 20 years' history in the educational sector, specialising in Creative Studies. Paul has combined his extensive experience of the media industry with his work with Awarding Organisations to become an established author and trainer.

Natalie Procter is Head of Media at Bishop Ullathorne RC High School and Humanities College as well as being the Course Organiser for BTEC Level 2 First Creative Media Production at City College Coventry. She studied Communication, Culture and Media at Coventry University, and has worked in the print industry, having specialised in journalism and TV.

Acknowledgements

The publisher and authors would like to thank the following individuals and organisations for permission to reproduce photographs:

(Key: b-bottom; c-centre; l-left; r-right; t-top)

Alamy Images: 141, 147, /Adam Burn 42, /Adrian Sherratt 60, 197, /Adrian Sherratt 60, 197, /Alex Segre 114, Angela Hampton Picture Library 18, /Art Directors & TRIP 82, /Bobo 179, /Craig Fleming 185, 185b, /Craig Fleming 185, 185b, /Craig Holmes 171, /Form Advertising 27, 32, fStop 70, /Hornbil Images 129, /Ian Francis 110, /Ian Shaw 38, /Imagebroker 128, Jeff Greenberg 1, 5, keith morris 24, /Marwood Jenkins 146, /T.M.O.Pictures 131

Getty Images: 113tc, 154, /Adrian Weinbrecht 191, 194, /Andy Crawford 158, /B.C. Moller 161, /Digital Vision 34t, /Gregg Segal 65, Iconica. 20b, /Image Source 136, /MLS 113, /Peter Dazeley 105, 109, Ryan McVay. 13, /UpperCut Images 77, 99, /Wire Image 57, 95t, /Wire Image 57, 95t, /Zigy Kaluzny-Charles Thatcher 63t; **Illustrated London News Picture Library:** 100

iStockphoto: 84, 201, brett lamb. aw_030, /Diane Diederich 116, Gawrav Sinha. 51, iofoto. 139, Kirsty Pargeter. aw_029, Nathan Jones. 203, Oksana Struk. 195

Kobal Collection Ltd: Studio Canal / Working Title / Aronowitz, Myles 20

Pearson Education Ltd: Gareth Boden 72, 115, Gareth Boden 72, 115, Jules Selmes 16, 79, Jules Selmes 16, 79, Lord & Leverett 25, Rob Judges 29, 193, Rob Judges 29, 193, Sophie Bluy 143, Steve Shott 7, Studio 8. Clark Wiseman 123

Photos.com: 3

Shutterstock: Apollofoto. 55, Ben Heys. 204, /David Davis 80, Flashon Studio. 103, /Gabi Moisa 86, /Grant Blakeman 112, IKO. 169, /James R. Martin 96, /János Gehring 31, 107, /János Gehring 31, 107, János Gehring 108, Karen Grigoryan. 204t, Lev Olkha. 119, /Mandy Godbehear 35, /Miodrag Gajic 199, /Monkey Business Images 95, Phase4Photography. 189, /Stanislav Komogorov 53, 63, stavklem. 84t, . Svetlana Larina 73, Tracy Whiteside. 112tl, /vgstudio 121, 124, /YAKOBCHUK VASYL 68, Yuri Arcurs. 209

SuperStock: /Image Source 34

Tresham College of Further and Higher Education 75

All other images © Pearson Education

The publisher and authors would like to thank the following individuals and organisations for permission to reproduce their materials:

- **p.14** Age of UK Facebook members pie chart reproduced by kind permission of http://www.clickymedia.co.uk/2010/01/facebook-user-statistics-january-2010/
- **p.44** Sample radio script, reproduced by kind permission of http://ruyasonic.com/prd_pre-prod.htm
- **p.46** Sample storyboards reproduced by kind permission of Clyde Williams/ftvstudy.com/Cairns State High School
- **p.58** Market share of jobs in the creative media sector pie chart reproduced under the terms of the Click-Use Licence. Source: National Statistics (Nomis: www.nomisweb.co.uk) . Crown copyright material is reproduced with the permission of the Controller Office of Public Sector Information (OPSI).
- **p.134** Storyboard, reproduced by kind permission of Oliver Casserly
- **p.134** Audio script for a play, reproduced by kind permission of David Hodgson
- **p.156** sample script and **p.181** running order, reproduced by kind permission of Mark Brown at Synergy 102.6FM

The publisher and authors would like to thank the following individuals and companies for their permission to feature materials about them in case studies:

- **p.10** MTV networks UK and Ireland
- **p.51** Neil Kulkarni
- **p.75** Paul Franklin
- **p.83** Andover Sound
- **p.85** BARB Ltd
- **p.88** BBC
- **p.93** BBC
- **p.94** Keira Knightley
- **p.96** Press Complaints Commission
- **p.103** Martin Rockley
- **p.129** Film London, the capital's film and media agency www.filmlondon.org.uk
- **p.162** Yatin Valand
- **p.166** Andy Shaw
- **p.209** Simon Richardson
- **p.220** John Whittaker (The Oxford Research Agency), and Alastair Williams (Mark Making)
- **p.221** Stuart Cox, and David Hunt (Lightning Fish)
- **p.222** Richard Healey (ITV), and Simon Clayton (Simon Clayton Design)
- **p.223** James Heinz

Every effort has been made to contact copyright holders of material reproduced in this book. Any omissions will be rectified in subsequent printings if notice is given to the publishers.

Internet Explorer, PowerPoint and Windows are registered trademarks of Microsoft Corporation in the United States and/or other countries.

FireWire, iMovie, iPhone, Keynote, Mac and Mac OS are trademarks of Apple Inc., registered in the U.S. and other countries.

Adobe, Acrobat, Adobe Audition, Adobe Premiere, Photoshop and Flash are either registered trademarks or trademarks of Adobe Systems Incorporated in the United States and/or other countries.

About your BTEC Level 2 First Creative Media Production

Choosing to study for a BTEC Level 2 First Creative Media Production qualification is a great decision to make for lots of reasons. Creative Media Production can lead into you into a whole range of professions and sectors and allows you to explore your creativity in many different ways.

Your BTEC Level 2 First in Creative Media Production is a **vocational** or **work-related** qualification. This doesn't mean that it will give you all the skills you need to do a job, but it does mean that you'll have the opportunity to gain specific knowledge, understanding and skills that are relevant to your chosen subject or area of work.

What will you be doing?

The qualification is structured into **mandatory units** (ones that you must do) and **optional units** (ones that you can choose to do). How many units you do and which ones you cover depend on the type of qualification you are working towards.

- BTEC Level 2 First **Certificate** in Creative Media Production: 1 mandatory unit and 1 optional unit
- BTEC Level 2 First **Extended Certificate** in Creative Media Production: 2 mandatory units and 2 optional units
- BTEC Level 2 First **Diploma** in Creative Media Production: 4 mandatory units and 4 optional units

Unit number	Credit value	Unit name	Mandatory or Optional
1	5	Research for creative media production	M
2	5	Communication techniques for creative media production	M
3	5	The creative media sector	M
4	5	Media audiences and products	M
5	10	Video production	O
6	10	Audio production	O
7	10	Print production	O
8	10	Interactive media production	O
9	10	Photography techniques	O
10	10	Animation techniques	O
11	10	Web authoring	O
12	10	Digital graphics for interactive and print-based media	O
13	10	2D Digital art for computer games	O
14	10	Deconstructing computer games	O
15	10	Computer games testing	O
16	10	2D Computer game engines	O
17	10	3D Computer game engines	O
18	10	Advertising production	O
19	10	Writing for the creative media	O
20	10	Factual production for the creative media	O
21	10	Creative media production project	O

How to use this book

This book is designed to help you through your BTEC Level 2 First Creative Media Production course. It has two sections:

- **Mandatory units** section with chapters covering each of the mandatory units, giving detailed information about each of the learning outcomes

- A **process** section that takes you through the creation process of investigation, pre-production, production, post-production and review, helping you to develop these skills in relation to your chosen specialism

This book contains many features that will help you use your skills and knowledge in work-related situations and assist you in getting the most from your course.

Introduction

These introductions give you a snapshot of what to expect from each unit – and what you should be aiming for by the time you finish it!

Assessment and grading criteria

This table explains what you must do to achieve each of the assessment criteria for each unit. For each assessment criterion, shown by the grade button **P1**, there is an assessment activity.

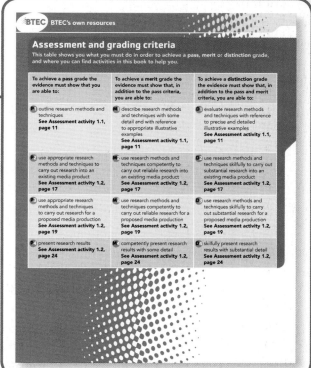

Assessment

Your teacher will set **assignments** throughout your course for you to complete. The assignments may focus on a particular type of product, and will require you to complete work for all the stages of developing a product. The important thing is that you evidence your skills and knowledge to date.

Stuck for ideas? Daunted by your first assignment? These students have all been through it before…

How you will be assessed

This unit will be assessed by a number of internal assignments designed to allow you to show your understanding of the unit outcomes. Most of the assignments that you will complete for this unit will relate to work that you are doing in some of your other units. This means that the research that you undertake will relate directly to the media products that you are studying and the media products that you are producing.

Your assessments could be in the form of:

* presentations
* case studies
* practical tasks
* written assignments.

Frank, Advertising production

This unit helped me to understand the things that I needed to do before I got my hands on the equipment to make my media product. It also showed me that all types of creative media production take careful planning and research to be successful.

I enjoyed using the internet and my centre's learning resource centre to find out more information about the films, television programmes and computer games that I like. It was good to do my own questionnaires, interviews and surveys and I became a lot more confident in talking to lots of different sorts of people. I even managed to run my own focus group, and was really surprised at the things I found out.

There were lots of practical tasks and activities for this unit, which made it more exciting for me. The bit I enjoyed most was planning and researching my own advertising production and gathering all of the material that I needed for it. It was great fun – and really interesting to see how all of my research material and information came together in the final production.

I was a little nervous about the final presentation of my research results as I had chosen to do this in front of an audience. However, it went really well and the positive feedback I got really boosted my confidence. Standing up and doing presentations in front of people is now not a problem. In fact, I love it!

* What areas of this unit might you find challenging?
* Which section of the unit are you most looking forward to?
* What preparation can you do in readiness for the unit assessments?

Activities

Assessment activities are suggestions for tasks that you might do as part of your assignment and will help you develop your knowledge, skills and understanding, Each of these has **grading tips** that clearly explain what you need to do in order to achieve a pass, merit or distinction.

BTEC Assessment activity 1.1

You are working as a researcher for a local media company and the boss has asked you to write a report for her about the different research methods and techniques that you could use in the role.

Think carefully about the two key methods of research you have learned about in this unit, the types of information they produce and the different research techniques that can be used.

1. In your own words, outline the main research methods and techniques. **P**
2. Describe the main research methods and techniques with some detail and include some examples of them being used. **M**
3. Evaluate the main research methods and techniques and include precise and detailed examples of them being used. **D**

Grading tips

To aim for a **merit** grade, you need to make some attempt to compare the different research methods and techniques. You should include examples of your own research as well as examples from within the creative media industries. You should also comment on the way in which your results were collated and how you stored the information safely.

To aim for a **distinction** grade, you should evaluate different research methods and techniques rather than just comparing them. This means that you should say something about the relative strengths and weaknesses of the different methods and techniques. Your examples will also need to be precise and detailed.

There are also suggestions for activities that will give you a broader grasp of the industry, stretch your imagination and deepen your skills.

Activity: Media research organisations

1. Visit the NRS and BARB websites and find out what information they have available about different media products. (See Hotlinks section on p. ii for links to their websites.)
2. Find out what other organisations undertake media research. Find out what information is available from them. Here are three to get you started:
   o Audit Bureau of Circulation (ABC)
   o Radio Joint Audience Research Limited (RAJAR)
   o Office of Communications (Ofcom)
3. Discuss what you have found out with the rest of the class.

Personal, learning and thinking skills

Throughout your BTEC First Creative Media Production course, there are lots of opportunities to develop your personal, learning and thinking skills. Look out for these as you progress.

PLTS

Collaborating with others and working towards common goals when undertaking research with other members of your class will help develop your skills as a **team worker**.

Functional skills

It's important that you have good English, maths and ICT skills – you never know when you'll need them, and employers will be looking for evidence that you've got these skills too.

Functional skills

Outlining the main research methods and techniques will help you to develop your **English** skills in writing.

Key terms

Technical words and phrases are easy to spot. You can also use the glossary at the back of the book.

Key term

Primary research – original research to obtain new information using techniques such as interviews, questionnaires and focus groups.

WorkSpace

Case studies provide snapshots of real workplace issues, and show how the skills and knowledge you develop during your course can help you in your career.

WorkSpace **Josh Zimsek**
Researcher

I am working on a short-term contract as a researcher with a local radio station. It is a bit like an apprenticeship as I am getting involved with lots of different tasks and meeting lots of different people.

I have to do boring things like making the tea and doing photocopying, but I also do more interesting things like searching on the Internet for information about guests who are coming on the programme. This research is very important as the presenters who interview guests on air need to know what questions to ask them.

I also do audience surveys to find out what our listeners think about us. Sometimes I will do this by asking questions over the telephone. Other times I will use a questionnaire and ask people in the street.

Being a researcher is all about information – knowing where to get it from and being able to get it quickly. You then have to check to make sure it is accurate and put it into the correct format and get it to the right person on time.

I have to work quickly and accurately and have good attention to detail. I also have to be a good communicator as I have to talk to lots of different types of people.

This is my first job in the industry and I am trying to make a good impression with the company so that I can get another contract with them or make sure they give me a good reference if I apply for a job with another company.

Think about it

1. What areas have you covered in this unit that provide you with the knowledge and skills needed by a researcher working within the creative media industries? Discuss with the rest of your class and produce a written summary of your key points.
2. What further skills might you need to develop in order to be successful in this role? Write a list and discuss what you have written with the rest of the class.
3. What do you think you need to do next to improve your chances of getting a job within a creative media industry? (Consider the courses you might do, e.g. National Diploma, where you might study, e.g. college or university, and work experience that could help you develop the right skills.)

Just checking

When you see this sort of activity, take stock! These quick activities and questions are there to check your knowledge. You can use them to see how much progress you've made or as a revision tool.

Edexcel's assignment tips

At the end of each chapter, you'll find hints and tips to help you get the best mark you can, such as the best websites to go to, checklists to help you remember processes and really useful facts and figures.

Have you read your **Level 2 BTEC First Study Skills Guide**? It's full of advice on study skills, putting your assignments together and making the most of being a BTEC Creative Media Production student.

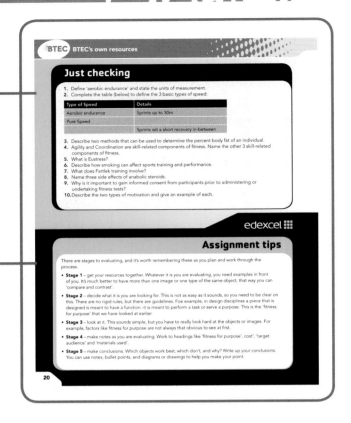

Just checking

1. Define 'aerobic endurance' and state the units of measurement.
2. Complete the table (below) to define the 3 basic types of speed:

Type of Speed	Details
Aerobic endurance	Sprints up to 30m
Pure Speed	
	Sprints wit a short recovery in-between

3. Describe two methods that can be used to determine the percent body fat of an individual.
4. Agility and Coordination are skill-related components of fitness. Name the other 3 skill-related components of fitness.
5. What is Eustress?
6. Describe how smoking can affect sports training and performance.
7. What does Fartlek training involve?
8. Name three side effects of anabolic steroids.
9. Why is it important to gain informed consent from participants prior to administering or undertaking fitness tests?
10. Describe the two types of motivation and give an example of each.

edexcel

Assignment tips

There are stages to evaluating, and it's worth remembering these as you plan and work through the process.

- **Stage 1** – get your resources together. Whatever it is you are evaluating, you need examples in front of you. It's much better to have more than one image or one type of the same object, that way you can 'compare and contrast'.
- **Stage 2** – decide what it is you are looking for. This is not as easy as it sounds, so you need to be clear on this. There are no rigid rules, but there are guidelines. Foe example, in design disciplines a piece that is designed to have a function -it is meant to perform a task or serve a purpose. This is the 'fitness for purpose' that we have looked at earlier.
- **Stage 3** – look at it. This sounds simple, but you have to really look hard at the objects or images. For example, factors like fitness for purpose are not always that obvious to see at first.
- **Stage 4** – make notes as you are evaluating. Work to headings like 'fitness for purpose', cost', 'target audience' and 'materials used'.
- **Stage 5** – make conclusions. Which objects work best, which don't, and why? Write up your conclusions. You can use notes, bullet points, and diagrams or drawings to help you make your point.

20

Ask your teacher about extra materials to help you through your course. You'll find interesting videos, activities, presentations and information about the Creative Media Production sector.

Your book is just part of the exciting resources from Edexcel to help you succeed in your BTEC course. Visit www.edexcel.com/BTEC or

www.pearsonfe.co.uk/BTEC 2010 for more details.

Credits: 5

1 Research for creative media production

The media world is bursting with creative media products trying to get our attention, and our money. Media producers put a lot of time and effort into planning and researching these creative media products.

The computer games, websites, television programmes, magazines and radio shows that we consume need to be carefully produced to appeal to the right audience. They need to generate enough income through sales, appeal to the right advertisers or sponsors, and attract a good size of audience to justify their position in today's competitive media market place. Researchers play a very important role in the creative process, and the information that they gather can change the content of the finished media product from the one that was originally planned.

This unit provides you with the opportunity to learn about the research methods and techniques that media producers use to try to make their creative media products a success. You will develop and use your research skills to investigate an existing media product that you are interested in. You will also research and gather material for your own creative media production. You will then have the opportunity to summarise your findings and present the results of your research.

Learning outcomes

After completing this unit you should:

1. know about research methods and techniques
2. be able to use research methods and techniques to investigate an existing media product
3. be able to use research methods and techniques to gather material for a media production
4. be able to present results of research.

Assessment and grading criteria

This table shows you what you must do in order to achieve a **pass**, **merit** or **distinction** grade, and where you can find activities in this book to help you.

To achieve a **pass** grade the evidence must show that you are able to:	To achieve a **merit** grade the evidence must show that, in addition to the pass criteria, you are able to:	To achieve a **distinction** grade the evidence must show that, in addition to the pass and merit criteria, you are able to:
P1 outline research methods and techniques **See Assessment activity 1.1, page 11**	**M1** describe research methods and techniques with some detail and with reference to appropriate illustrative examples **See Assessment activity 1.1, page 11**	**D1** evaluate research methods and techniques with reference to precise and detailed illustrative examples **See Assessment activity 1.1, page 11**
P2 use appropriate research methods and techniques to carry out research into an existing media product **See Assessment activity 1.2, page 17**	**M2** use research methods and techniques competently to carry out reliable research into an existing media product **See Assessment activity 1.2, page 17**	**D2** use research methods and techniques skilfully to carry out substantial research into an existing media product **See Assessment activity 1.2, page 17**
P3 use appropriate research methods and techniques to carry out research for a proposed media production **See Assessment activity 1.2, page 19**	**M3** use research methods and techniques competently to carry out reliable research for a proposed media production **See Assessment activity 1.2, page 19**	**D3** use research methods and techniques skilfully to carry out substantial research for a proposed media production **See Assessment activity 1.2, page 19**
P4 present research results **See Assessment activity 1.2, page 24**	**M4** competently present research results with some detail **See Assessment activity 1.2, page 24**	**D4** skilfully present research results with substantial detail **See Assessment activity 1.2, page 24**

How you will be assessed

This unit will be assessed by a number of internal assignments designed to allow you to show your understanding of the unit outcomes. Most of the assignments that you will complete for this unit will relate to work that you are doing in some of your other units. This means that the research that you undertake will relate directly to the media products that you are studying and the media products that you are producing.

Your assessments could be in the form of:

* presentations
* case studies
* practical tasks
* written assignments.

Frank, Advertising production

This unit helped me to understand the things that I needed to do before I got my hands on the equipment to make my media product. It also showed me that all types of creative media production take careful planning and research to be successful.

I enjoyed using the internet and my centre's learning resource centre to find out more information about the films, television programmes and computer games that I like. It was good to do my own questionnaires, interviews and surveys and I became a lot more confident in talking to lots of different sorts of people. I even managed to run my own focus group, and was really surprised at the things I found out.

There were lots of practical tasks and activities for this unit, which made it more exciting for me. The bit I enjoyed most was planning and researching my own advertising production and gathering all of the material that I needed for it. It was great fun – and really interesting to see how all of my research material and information came together in the final production.

I was a little nervous about the final presentation of my research results as I had chosen to do this in front of an audience. However, it went really well and the positive feedback I got really boosted my confidence. Standing up and doing presentations in front of people is now not a problem. In fact, I love it!

* What areas of this unit might you find challenging?
* Which section of the unit are you most looking forward to?
* What preparation can you do in readiness for the unit assessments?

1. Know about research methods and techniques

Set up

Favourite television programme

What is your favourite television programme at the moment?

Write down the different methods you could use to find out the answers to these questions about your favourite television programme.

- How many people in your class watch this programme?
- What do they think about it?
- How many people in the UK watch it?
- Is it more popular with girls or with boys?

Discuss your findings with the rest of the class and then use the best suggestions to find out some of the answers.

To be able to undertake successful research for creative media production you need to have a good understanding of the main research methods and techniques that are used within the industry.

When you carry out your own research later in this unit you will need to use both **primary** and **secondary** research methods.

Primary research

The first question about your favourite television programme should have been easy for you to answer, but to answer the others you will need to do some **primary research**. Primary research is original research that is undertaken to find out new information. This involves asking people questions. The main techniques used by researchers when conducting primary research are asking people to complete a questionnaire, interviewing people in the street or over the phone, or running a focus group.

Key term

Primary research – original research to obtain new information using techniques such as interviews, questionnaires and focus groups.

Did you know?

Recent primary research in America showed that 52% of teenagers played computer games that involved thinking about moral and ethical issues, 43% played games in which they made decisions about how a community, city or nation should be run, and 40% played games where they learned about a social issue.

Computer game designers will use information like this to help them plan, design and produce a computer game that will appeal to a teenage audience.

In the creative media sector, a film company, television producer or games developer will show a preview of their new product to a group of people, often called a focus group, and ask them what they think of it. The answers that the focus group give often lead to changes being made to the product before it is launched.

Activity: Producing a simple questionnaire

1. In small groups, discuss what media-related information you would like to find out about the rest of the class. You might want to find out:
   o the most popular games console in the class and the top five games played
   o the radio station that people listen to and their favourite DJ
   o the number of times people visit the cinema and what film they saw last
   o how many people have satellite television and how many hours they watch in an average week
   o which social networking site people use and how many contacts they have on it.
2. Produce a simple questionnaire that your group can use with other members of the class to find out this information.
3. After completing the questionnaire, collate the results and discuss the findings with the rest of the class.

PLTS

Collaborating with others when working on your questionnaire will help develop your skills as a **team worker.**

Functional skills

Producing the questionnaire will help you to develop your **English** skills in writing.

Using a questionnaire is an example of a primary research technique. Which primary research techniques have you used?

Secondary research

Sometimes a media organisation will decide to use research information that has already been gathered and analysed by somebody else. This is called **secondary research**. Secondary research techniques include finding information from books, magazines and archive material, searching for information on the Internet and taking notes from research studies that have already been undertaken.

A media organisation will often use secondary research to save time and to add to their own primary research. They will also use it to help them prove that what they are saying is true. For example, a magazine publisher might want to prove to an advertiser that their magazine really is read by thousands of teenage boys, and will use information from an organisation such as the National Readership Survey (NRS) to support what they are saying.

Key term

Secondary research – research using information already gathered by other people or organisations. Often available in books, magazines or websites.

Did you know?

Media research organisations such as the National Readership Survey (NRS) and the Broadcasters' Audience Research Board (BARB) undertake primary research of their own and then sell the results to other media companies. This information is then used as secondary research to add to any primary research that media companies carry out themselves.

Activity: Media research organisations

1. Visit the NRS and BARB websites and find out what information they have available about different media products. (See Hotlinks section on p. ii for links to their websites.)
2. Find out what other organisations undertake media research. Find out what information is available from them. Here are three to get you started:
   o Audit Bureau of Circulation (ABC)
   o Radio Joint Audience Research Limited (RAJAR)
   o Office of Communications (Ofcom)
3. Discuss what you have found out with the rest of the class.

Quantitative and qualitative information

When you undertake your own research you will obtain two main sorts of information. The first is called **quantitative** and the second is called **qualitative**.

Quantitative information can be measured and counted. It can usually be shown as a set of numbers and is often presented in the form of tables, charts and diagrams.

Both primary and secondary research methods can produce quantitative information. Media companies need information on how many people are reading their magazines and newspapers, watching their films and television programmes, clicking on their websites and listening to their musical products. Factual information about ratings, circulation and viewing figures, website hits and market analysis can all be represented as quantitative data, see Figure 1.1 on p. 7.

Key terms

Quantitative research – research based on measurable facts and information that can be counted, producing numerical and statistical data.

Qualitative research – research that is based on opinions, attitudes and preferences, rather than facts and figures.

Qualitative information is more subjective and is concerned with people's opinions, views and preferences. Both primary and secondary research methods can produce qualitative information. It is often very important within the creative media sector as it is used to find out what individuals and groups think and feel about a particular media product.

The results of qualitative research are often more difficult to analyse than quantitative data and the information is often difficult to represent statistically, particularly if the responses are personal and subjective.

Table 1.1: Responses from a sample of teenagers surveyed about their thoughts about a social networking site.

Name	Response
Rob	I really liked the site and found it easy to use. Colours were bright and made me feel very positive. I will probably visit it again.
Siobhan	Hated it. Too busy. Colours too bright. Difficult to navigate around. Won't be using it again.
Raj	Loved the design, but found it a bit tricky to use. Prefer Bebo. Lots of information. Colours reminded me of the countryside. Overall I like it and will visit again.

When a computer game company asks a focus group what they think about a new game they are about to launch, it is likely they will receive both quantitative and qualitative information. The following are some examples.

- Before playing the game the group fills out a short questionnaire. The results show that 75% of the boys and 48% of the girls regularly play this type of computer game. This is quantitative data.

- After playing the game, the company asks each individual what they thought about it. What did they think about the graphics? What were their feelings about the main characters? What did they understand about the storyline? How did the gameplay compare with other games that they have played? These questions will provide qualitative information.

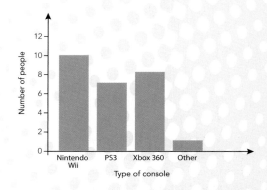

Figure 1.1: Type of games console owned by people in a class. This is quantitative data. What type of games console do you have at home?

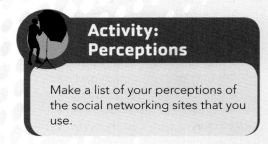

Activity: Perceptions

Make a list of your perceptions of the social networking sites that you use.

Think about it

What impact have computers and the Internet had on the way in which we communicate?

What's your favourite computer game? Why?

Activity: Different types of questions

1. Which of the questions below will produce quantitative data?
2. Which of the questions below will produce qualitative data?
   a) Are you male or female?
   b) Which age range are you in?
      Under 16, 16–19, 20–25, Over 25
   c) What are your thoughts about getting old?
   d) Are you thinking about going to university when you are older?
   e) How do you feel about going to university?
   f) What job would you like to do in the future?

Research techniques

One of the skills needed in planning an effective research project is the ability to choose the right research techniques so that you can get the correct information. Remember that some techniques are used in primary research and others are used in secondary research, and most can be used to gather both qualitative and quantitative information.

Table 1.2: Advantages and disadvantages of research methods.

Research technique	Primary or secondary	Advantage	Disadvantage	Can be used to...
Using the library/reading	Secondary	Wide range of information available	Can be time-consuming and involve a lot of searching for the right information	Find reliable, published information on media products and for the content of media productions
Using the Internet	Secondary	Can quickly find a lot of information. Easy to download and print material. Able to undertake searches for specific information	Some sources not always reliable. Can produce too much information, some of which is not relevant	Find information on media products and for the content of media productions
Searching archives	Secondary	Good for historical information	Information can be outdated	Find information on old media products and for the content of media productions
Interviews	Primary	Quick way of getting people's views and opinions about things	Easy to forget what people have said so need to record interview	Find out what people think about something. The interviews might be good enough to be in the media product itself
Observations	Primary	Easy way of seeing for yourself what is happening	Can be limited information as it is only your opinion	Researching for a media production

Activity: Choosing the correct research techniques

The table below contains more research techniques. Copy and complete the table to help you decide on the best techniques to use for your own research projects.

Research technique	Primary or secondary	Advantage	Disadvantage	Can be used to...
Questionnaires/surveys	Primary			Find out what people think about something
Focus group				
Recce (see p. 127)		Helps you to plan how you are going to do the actual production Makes you aware of potential problems in advance	Can be time-consuming	Research a media production

Information trail

You need to be organised when you are undertaking your own research and it helps to have a record of the information trail that you have followed. The best way of doing this is to keep a log of all of the library, Internet and archive searches that you have undertaken whilst carrying out your research.

Figure 1.2 shows an extract from a research log that details the information trail undertaken by a Creative Media Production learner when researching for one of her own media products.

Research log

Project: Gathering materials for documentary on healthy eating

Date	Source of information	Description of information obtained	Notes
12/9/10	Website: www.eatwell.gov.uk	Information about healthy diet 8 tips for eating well Food myths	Good, reliable source of government information. Can be used as captions in final video
13/9/10	Website: www.bbc.co.uk/health	What makes a balanced diet Food needs for different age groups	Another reliable source. Age information is good to use and we can select right info for our target audience
13/9/10	Book: Romanoff J, The Eating Well Healthy in a Hurry Cookbook, (Norton 2005)	Healthy food recipes	Good recipes but not suitable for our target audience
14/9/10	Interview with Mrs Foxton the school cook	Lots of information about cooking meals for target age group	Be good to record an interview with her for the documentary. Consent form would need to be signed.
14/9/10	Recce of canteen area	Suitable locations identified (see photographs in research folder)	Health and safety would need to be checked and approval from head

Figure 1.2: Extract from a research log. What information do you include in your research log?

Collating and storing research material

The amount of information that you will gather when undertaking your own research can be very large, particularly when it is linked to one of your own creative media productions, and you will need to collate and store your research material.

Collating your research material involves sifting through all of the material to identify what is useful and what needs to be disregarded. Sort your material into useful categories that will help you to find it easily at a later date. Once you have done this, you need to log, organise and store your research material in a safe and secure way.

It is good practice to create a research folder in which you can store all of your relevant research material. It needs to have a clear index system so that you can easily find a relevant piece of information. Any secondary material that is stored should be highlighted and annotated so it is clear what you have selected from it and what it has been used for.

It is also good to include some form of written commentary in your file that explains to the tutor and moderator what is in there, how it was obtained, why it has been included and how it has been used.

> ### Remember
>
> Quality is better than quantity. Many learners put all of the research material that they have produced into a folder and expect to receive a good mark for it. Make sure you submit only useful and relevant material. It is not good practice to submit a research folder filled with pages and pages downloaded from the Internet, with little or no relevance to the project being carried out.

Case study: MTV online

MTV has become a household name, supplying cable and satellite viewers with a range of television music channels that has grown since the launch of the first MTV channel over 20 years ago.

MTV's target audience is clearly defined, and helped to develop the concept of 'youth television'. When it wanted to develop an online Internet presence it didn't want to assume that what worked for its established television audience would also be successful for its new online users.

The company knew how many people were accessing the site by counting the number of hits, but this figure didn't tell them anything about the people themselves. To find out more, the company devised a questionnaire that asked people about their hobbies and interests, and what they spent on music devices, clothes and going out. The questionnaire was placed on the MTV website, along with an incentive to win CDs for a few lucky winners drawn out of a hat.

The questionnaire proved to be very popular (particularly with the incentive to win CDs) and the company soon had a mountain of information to sift through and collate. By sorting through it carefully

and collating it into different categories they were able to produce a detailed profile of their online target audience. The main focus of this research was the youth market; because one of the first questions asked the respondents to put themselves into an age category they were able to disregard the replies from older people.

By putting site users into different categories, MTV was able to examine lifestyle habits and compare them to site usage patterns. For example, they found that the average 18-year-old female who prefers R&B to house music might spend £50 a month on CDs, whereas the male equivalent might prefer to spend £50 a month on DVDs. This kind of information allows MTV to target these individual groups of users more efficiently.

- The incentive to win CDs worked for them at the time. Why might this be less successful now?
- What other incentives do you think would work better if they were to carry out a similar survey today?
- Why would the information that MTV obtained be very useful for potential advertisers?

Research material can be very sensitive, particularly if it contains people's personal views about something, and they might be very unhappy if it is made public or the wrong person sees it. The Data Protection Act is a law that says that anyone who handles personal information has to be very careful about how it is stored and who has access to it.

Activity: The Data Protection Act

Do some research of your own to find out more information about the Data Protection Act.

The website of the Information Commissioner's Office is a good starting point. (See Hotlinks section on p. ii for a link to this website.)

Research information is also bought and sold by media companies and can be very valuable to them. They will try to keep the information as secure as possible to stop one of their rivals getting their hands on it and using it to their advantage.

Think about it

What information do you think should be kept private?

Assessment activity 1.1 P1 M1 D1

You are working as a researcher for a local media company and the boss has asked you to write a report for her about the different research methods and techniques that you could use in the role.

Think carefully about the two key methods of research you have learned about in this unit, the types of information they produce and the different research techniques that can be used.

1. In your own words, outline the main research methods and techniques. **P1**

2. Describe the main research methods and techniques with some detail and include some examples of them being used. **M1**

3. Evaluate the main research methods and techniques and include precise and detailed examples of them being used. **D1**

Grading tips

To aim for a **merit** grade, you need to make some attempt to compare the different research methods and techniques. You should include examples of your own research as well as examples from within the creative media industries. You should also comment on the way in which your results were collated and how you stored the information safely.

To aim for a **distinction** grade, you should evaluate different research methods and techniques rather than just comparing them. This means that you should say something about the relative strengths and weaknesses of the different methods and techniques. Your examples will also need to be precise and detailed.

PLTS

Collaborating with others and working towards common goals when undertaking research with other members of your class will help develop your skills as a **team worker**.

Functional skills

Outlining the main research methods and techniques will help you to develop your **English** skills in writing.

2. Be able to use research methods and techniques to investigate an existing media product

When planning what research you are going to undertake for this learning outcome it is a good idea to link it with the work that you are doing in some of your other units, particularly Unit 3 The creative media sector or Unit 4 Media audiences and products. In these two units you will already be looking at and analysing specific media products and it is good practice to choose one of these products for the investigation for this unit.

Activity: Choosing your media product

1. In small groups discuss the work that you are doing in your other units. Draw up a list of potential media products that you could investigate further for this unit.

2. Discuss the advantages and disadvantages of each product, writing down the key points as they are discussed.

3. Summarise the key points of the discussion and decide which product each member of the group is going to investigate further.

Examples of media products that you could investigate for this unit include:

- a local or national newspaper
- a lifestyle or hobby magazine
- a television programme
- a film or DVD
- a social networking website
- a computer game
- a radio programme.

This list gives only some of the examples and it is best if you discuss the options with your tutor and pick an existing media product that you are interested in.

You should aim to use both primary and secondary research methods when investigating an existing media product and obtain both quantitative and qualitative information.

You might use books and the Internet to find out some factual information about your product, such as who its target audience is and how much it costs to produce. You might then design a questionnaire or organise a focus group to find out what a sample of the audience thinks and feels about the product

Purpose of research

Before undertaking any research it is important that you understand what the main purpose of the research is. One of the main reasons that media companies pay for and undertake their own research is to gather information about the audience for particular media products. They are interested in the composition of the audience, its size and how the audience reacts to and feels about the product.

The composition of the audience for the product that you are investigating should be an important focus of your research for this learning outcome as media companies will design their products for a specific target audience.

When undertaking research, media producers describe their target audience by age, gender, culture and social class.

Age

The age of the target audience is important because some kinds of product can only be shown to or bought by certain age groups.

The British Board of Film Classification (bbfc) puts an age category on all films (shown at the cinema and available on DVD) that are available in the UK. Computer games are now given an age classification by the Pan-European Game Information (PEGI) system.

Many advertisers are also interested in what different age groups are reading, watching and interacting with as they can then decide whether or not to advertise their products within particular media products.

Who is your target market? How will you make your product appeal to them?

Age of UK Facebook members, January 2010

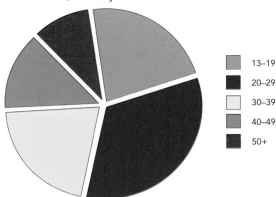

- 13–19
- 20–29
- 30–39
- 40–49
- 50+

Figure 1.3: This chart shows the age breakdown of UK Facebook members. What products do you think would be suitable to promote on the website?

For example, Figure 1.3 shows the age of UK members of the social networking site Facebook in January 2010. It shows that, at the time, the website was most popular with people between the ages of 20 and 29. A potential advertiser would be interested in this information so that it can decide what products to promote on the site and the best way to do so.

Gender

Gender is also an important category to media companies as many media products are targeted at either men or women. This is most clearly seen within the magazine market, which has specific magazines targeted at males and others targeted at females.

Culture

People's needs and wants as consumers will also vary according to their culture, language and background, and many media products are available that target people from a particular cultural background.

The media industry is now very much a global one and newspapers, magazines, radio and television programmes from all over the world are readily available to people living in the UK.

Activity: Magazines for men and women

In small groups, look at a selection of magazines and write down the main features that help to target each one at either men or women.

Can you think of any magazines that target both men and women?

There is a growing production base in Britain for media products that target different cultures and ethnic groups. What different groups of people might a media product in your local area want to target?

Social class

You can also categorise an audience according to a rough idea about their social class. Social class is often linked to a person's income, which can be important for advertisers. For example, it is no good advertising an expensive top-of-the-range sports car to people who are unemployed or have a low disposable income.

Most companies involved with media research and production use a scale that puts people into categories according to the sort of job they do and the amount of income that they have. The scale is a very rough one and does make some very broad assumptions about what people earn.

Table 1.3: Rough guide to social status according to occupation.

Social grade	Social status	Chief income earner's occupation
A	Upper middle class	Higher managerial, administrative or professional
B	Middle class	Intermediate managerial, administrative or professional
C1	Lower middle class	Supervisory or clerical and junior managerial, administrative or professional
C2	Skilled working class	Skilled manual workers
D	Working class	Semi and unskilled manual workers
E	Those at the lowest levels of subsistence	State pensioners, casual or lowest grade workers

Activity: Newspaper readership

The table below shows the readership of two popular national newspapers according to their social class. What does this tell you about the content of the two papers? What features and advertisements are you most likely to find in each of the papers?

Title	AB	C1	C2	DE
The Guardian	60%	30%	5%	5%
The Sun	11%	23%	30%	36%

Think about it

Which other sources of news are available to you?

Comparing similar products

As well as looking at audiences, media companies are also interested in comparing similar products. A games design company looking to launch a new computer game needs to know what other products are on the market so that it doesn't produce one that is too similar to an existing one.

They will, however, be interested in knowing what the most popular games are at the moment, and they might want to launch a similar type of game that can also cash in on that trend.

Activity: Types of computer games

In small groups write down the different types of computer games (sports games, role play, adventure, etc.) and then try to think of at least five specific examples of each type that are currently available.

Which is the most popular one in each category? What makes it so popular? Are the other ones trying to copy the most popular one or are they trying to break new ground?

Investigating production processes

A media company will also be interested in how other media products are produced and what techniques and technologies are being used. The way a product looks and sounds can be very important, particularly if the target audience is young and fashion-conscious. The last thing a company will want to produce is a product that looks stale and old-fashioned.

Activity: Evolving products

As audience expectations change and production processes develop, so do the media products themselves. For example, a magazine aimed at teenage girls today looks very different to the ones produced in the 1970s, and will contain very different issues and articles. Can you think of any other examples of products that have changed over the years?

Think about the magazines you read. What features appeal to you and what would you change?

 **Assessment activity 1.2** **P2 M2 D2**

You work as a freelance researcher and have been approached by a creative media production company to help them with some research. They are gathering information about a specific sector of the market and have asked you to help them by investigating a particular media product within this sector.

1. Plan the research methods and techniques that you are going to use to investigate the chosen media product.

2. Undertake the investigation, using both primary and secondary research methods to obtain quantitative and qualitative data.

3. Collate and organise your research material and analyse the results.

Grading tips

To aim for a **merit** grade, you need to choose carefully which research techniques and methods you will use and have a clear idea about what you are trying to find out. You will need to sort through the information gathered and decide what you are going to keep and what you can discard. Store the material that you select so that you can easily find a specific piece of information

To aim for a **distinction** grade, you need to show a clear sense of purpose in carrying out your research and use appropriate procedures and techniques to good effect. You will need to work carefully and methodically to produce a substantial amount of material from a wide range of sources. All information obtained should be evaluated and sifted, and the relevant material stored in such a way that any given piece of information is easily traceable.

 PLTS

Planning and carrying out your research into an existing media product will help you to develop your skills as an **independent enquirer**.

 Functional skills

Undertaking secondary research via the Internet when investigating a media product will help you to develop your **ICT** skills in selecting and using a variety of sources of information.

3. Be able to use research methods and techniques to gather material for a media production

When you are planning the work for this learning outcome it is good practice to gather material for one of the media productions that you are undertaking in one of the optional practical units. For example:

- you can use the skills and knowledge that you have developed in this unit to help you to research and gather material for the video product that you are going to make in Unit 5 Video production

- you could choose to gather material for a production you are undertaking in Unit 6 Audio production, Unit 7 Print production, Unit 8 Interactive media production or Unit 18 Advertising production, among others.

 Activity: Choosing your production project

Discuss what practical production units you are doing with the rest of your class. Write down a list of the practical projects that you will be working on. Discuss the options with your tutor and write down the issues that you would need to consider for each one.

Think about what you want to find out from your interviewees. How will you record their responses?

Whichever unit you choose, the process of gathering material will be very similar and you will need to use both primary and secondary research methods, and obtain both quantitative and qualitative information.

You might use books and the Internet to find out more about the production processes involved and the technology you will need to use. You might also use the Internet, magazines and books to gather information for the actual content of your production. Interviewing people is another good way of getting information to include in your media production.

 Think about it

If you are planning to produce a student magazine for Unit 7, what type of features or articles could you include in the magazine? Where could you get the information to help you write the stories?

You will need to target your media production at the right audience and find out what that audience expects to find in the product that you are going to make. You will need to survey a sample of your target audience and use some primary research techniques to gather this information.

Assessment activity 1.3

P3 **M3** **D3**

You work for a local media production company that is planning to launch a new product onto the market. You have been asked to use your skills as a researcher to help gather material for the new media production.

1. Think carefully about the production that you will be undertaking and put together a plan of the different research methods and techniques that you are going to use to gather material for the media production. You should plan to use both primary and secondary research methods to obtain both quantitative and qualitative information.

2. Carry out the research to gather the material that you will need for the production.

3. Carefully sift through the material, discarding what you do not need, and then collate and organise it so that you can easily access it during the pre-production and production stages.

4. Analyse your results.

Grading tips

To aim for a **merit** grade, you need to choose your research techniques and methods carefully and have a clear idea about what you are trying to find out. You will need to sort through the information gathered and decide what you are going to keep and what you can discard. The material that is finally selected will need to be stored in such a way that it can be easily accessed so it is easy to find a specific piece of information.

To aim for a **distinction** grade, you need to show a clear sense of purpose in carrying out your research and use appropriate procedures and techniques to good effect. You will need to work carefully and methodically to produce a substantial amount of material from a wide range of sources. All information obtained will be evaluated and sifted, and the relevant material stored in such a way that any given piece of information is easily traceable.

PLTS

Asking questions to extend your thinking when trying out alternative ways of researching for a proposed media production will help you to develop your skills as a **creative thinker.**

Functional skills

Collating and storing your research material on a computer will help you to develop your **ICT** skills in managing information storage.

4. Be able to present results of research

You will have completed at least two pieces of research for this unit and you now have the opportunity to present the results of this research and summarise what you have learned.

Format

You can present the results of your research in the form of a written report, as an oral presentation to the rest of the class or in an audio-visual format. If you do an oral presentation you could include slides produced in a presentation graphics program to help structure and support what you are saying and undertake the presentation on your own or as part of a group. Discuss the options with your tutor and decide which format is best for you.

If you choose to present your findings in the form of a presentation, you must make sure that it is recorded so that your mark can be checked by the moderator towards the end of the course. Many job interviews now include giving a presentation to a panel of people, so presenting the results of your research in this way is good practice for you.

What would be the best way of presenting your research?

Content

Whichever format you choose to present the results of your research, you need to make sure that you include all of the following required content:

- An introduction to your research project in which you explain clearly what the purpose of the reseach was. In other words, what exactly were you trying to find out and why were you doing it?

- A section in which you describe and explain the research methods and techniques that you used in your research project, and the procedures that you carried out.

- A summary of the data that you obtained, presented in a form that is easy to understand. You might want to use a selection of graphs, charts and tables to help you do this.

- A section in which you explain and analyse the results that you obtained, and draw some conclusions. What did the results of your research show? Did you expect these results or were some of them a surprise to you? Do these results change your views on what you were researching? How will you use these results?

- A summary of the sources that you have used, including a **bibliography** of any published works. When referencing books, include:
  - the author's surname followed by his or her initial
  - the title of the book, which is often written in italics or in bold
  - the name of the publisher and the year that it was published in brackets

  For example:

  Berger, A – *Media Research Techniques, 2nd Edition* (Sage, 1998).

  You should also include a list of other sources you have used such as newspapers, magazines and websites.

When creating a presentation, think carefully about the contents of each slide:

- Don't cram in too much – brief bullet points will get your message across more clearly than a full page of text.

- Each slide should provide a summary of what you are saying rather than a running commentary.

Expression

The way in which you communicate the results of your research to your audience is very important if they are to understand fully what you are telling them. Table 1.4 on p. 22 shows four key factors that you need to think about: they are important whichever format you choose to present your results in.

Key term

Bibliography – a list of books that you have used in your research project.

 Remember

Don't be tempted to use too many visual and sound effects with your slides as the audience will easily tire of gimmicks. They can also distract from your message.

Table 1.4: Key factors to consider when presenting your results.

Key factor	What it means	Top tips
Structure	The order in which you present your results and the way in which you divide it up into different sections.	Use a logical order when presenting your results: • Start with an outline of what you were trying to find out. • Explain your research process. • Show the results. • Explain what you did with the results and what impact it had. Use sub-headings to help to structure your report or presentation.
Clarity	To be successful you have to be clear in what you say. This means having a clear plan from the start and explaining what you did and found out in a straightforward way that your audience will understand.	Have a clear plan of what you are going to say and stick to it. Practise and record your presentation so that you can watch it. Make sure you can understand it and your meaning is clear. Draft and redraft your written report and check the final version so that it makes sense.
Register	This refers to the actual words used, whether spoken or written, and how technical or formal you want to sound.	Don't use words that are too technical or will confuse your audience. Think carefully about your words: too informal ('Alright mates') or too formal ('Good morning ladies and gentlemen') might set you off on the wrong footing. A simple but straightforward 'Hello and welcome to my presentation' might be a better way to start.
Audience	You will need to have a good understanding of who is in your audience and make sure your language, structure and content is appropriate for them.	Don't assume that your audience already knows what you have done. Remember that your work may well be looked at by somebody from outside your centre who hasn't seen you working throughout the year, and they will need to be able to understand what you have done from the work that you present to them.

Think about it

Think about your communication skills:

- How confident are you when talking in front of a group of people?
- What can you do to improve the way in which you get your ideas across?
- What about your writing skills?
- Do you need help in structuring and organising your written work?

Activity: Recording yourself

Practise different ways of delivering your spoken language. Record the results and then listen back to see what you sound like. Be warned: your recorded voice will sound very different from what you are used to hearing.

- What do you sound like?
- Do you speak too quickly?
- Do you sound confident?
- What can you do to improve the way in which you deliver your spoken language?

Case study: Shenica's presentation

Shenica is a learner doing the First Diploma in Creative Media Production. She decided to deliver the results of her research in the form of a presentation to her classmates.

Her tutor was also in the audience so he could assess what she had done, and he had arranged for one of the other members of the class to record the presentation on video tape so that he had a record of the work that he could then show to the moderator at the end of the course.

Shenica was quite nervous about the presentation because she had never really talked in front of an audience before. However, she had prepared what she was going to say beforehand and had done a run through at home in front of her friends.

She decided to structure her talk using slides produced in the PowerPoint® presentation graphics program so that she always knew where she was in her presentation and knew what came next.

She also decided to hand out some of the graphs that she had produced from her survey results and to ask the class, in pairs, to look at the graphs and try to work out what they were showing.

Despite a nervous start, Shenica soon grew in confidence and was actually starting to enjoy it towards the end. She asked the audience some questions in the middle of the presentation to add some variety and to check that they were paying attention. The presentation went very well, and the rest of the class said that they had learnt a lot from her talk and liked the way she had presented the information to them in the form of the graphs.

- What slides would you produce to help to structure your presentation?
- Do you have data that you could present in the form of a graph or a chart?
- What questions would you ask your audience to help keep them engaged?

Follow this checklist to make sure you have a successful presentation.

- Plan what you are going to say and have a set of cue cards ready to remind you.

- Practice makes perfect, so make sure that you do a complete run through before the big day.

- Dress to impress by looking smart.

- Think carefully about your body language and try to communicate a confident attitude to your audience.

- Try to look at each member of your audience at least once during the presentation. This will make them feel at ease.

- Use PowerPoint® slides to summarise what you are saying. Keep the words short and simple and don't be tempted simply to read from the slides.

- Ask the audience questions to get them engaged and keep them interested.

- Summarise your main points at the end of the presentation.

- Thank your audience for listening and invite any final questions.

Assessment activity 1.4 P4 M4 D4

You need to present the results of the following two main research studies that you completed for this unit:

- **Your investigation into an existing media product.**
- **Your research for one of your own media productions.**

1. Discuss the options with your tutor and decide what format you will use to present the results for each of the two research studies.

2. Gather all of the research material that you have produced and make sure that it is collated, organised and stored securely.

3. Work on the content of your report or presentation, making sure that you cover all of the required aspects.

4. Complete the final report or deliver the final presentation.

Grading tips

To aim for a **merit** grade, the summary of your research should be more than a simple outline of what you did. You should include some detailed description of the research methods and techniques used and some detail of the results obtained.

To aim for a **distinction** grade, you should provide a full account of the research methods and techniques undertaken and precise details of the results obtained.

PLTS

Inviting feedback on your presentations and dealing positively with praise, setbacks and criticism will help you become a more **reflective learner**.

Functional skills

Developing the presentations of your research will help you to improve your **ICT** skills in entering, developing and formatting information.

Practise your presentation in a mirror, in front of your family, or record yourself. What improvements could you make to your delivery?

I am working on a short-term contract as a researcher with a local radio station. It is a bit like an apprenticeship as I am getting involved with lots of different tasks and meeting lots of different people.

I have to do boring things like making the tea and doing photocopying, but I also do more interesting things like searching on the Internet for information about guests who are coming on the programme. This research is very important as the presenters who interview guests on air need to know what questions to ask them.

I also do audience surveys to find out what our listeners think about us. Sometimes I will do this by asking questions over the telephone. Other times I will use a questionnaire and ask people in the street.

Being a researcher is all about information – knowing where to get it from and being able to get it quickly. You then have to check to make sure it is accurate and put it into the correct format and get it to the right person on time.

I have to work quickly and accurately and have good attention to detail. I also have to be a good communicator as I have to talk to lots of different types of people.

This is my first job in the industry and I am trying to make a good impression with the company so that I can get another contract with them or make sure they give me a good reference if I apply for a job with another company.

Think about it

1. What areas have you covered in this unit that provide you with the knowledge and skills needed by a researcher working within the creative media industries? Discuss with the rest of your class and produce a written summary of your key points.

2. What further skills might you need to develop in order to be successful in this role? Write a list and discuss what you have written with the rest of the class.

3. What do you think you need to do next to improve your chances of getting a job within a creative media industry? (Consider the courses you might do, e.g. National Diploma, where you might study, e.g. college or university, and work experience that could help you develop the right skills.)

Just checking

1. What are the two main methods of research used in the creative media industries?
2. What are the two main types of information that a researcher will aim to gather?
3. List the main research techniques that you can use when gathering information about a media product.
4. Which practical units link well with this unit when you need to gather some information for a media production?
5. What four categories are commonly used to divide up a target audience?
6. What is the name of the organisation that classifies films and DVDs?
7. What system is used to put an age classification on computer games?
8. What are the six main social grades used to classify media audiences?
9. What does 'register' mean?
10. What is a bibliography?
11. What makes a successful presentation?

Assignment tips

- Try to get some practical experience of using the different research methods and techniques. This will make it easier for you to talk about them when you do the assessment activity for LO1.

- Link the research that you do for LO2 and LO3 to the work that you are already doing in your other units. This will make the research more meaningful to you and will save you valuable time.

- Carefully sift through the research material that you have gathered and try to make a judgement as to what is important and what is not. Do not be tempted to include all of your research material in your final portfolio. Quantity is not the same as quality!

- Think carefully about the way in which you present the results of your research. Don't assume that your audience already knows what you are trying to achieve.

- It is often better to present quantitative data in the form of tables, graphs or charts. This can be a visually appealing way of showing complex information more clearly.

- Check through all of your work before you finally submit it. A well-organised folder that has a logical structure, is clear in what it is trying to say and is well written with no spelling mistakes will make a good impression.

2 Communication techniques for creative media production

This unit is concerned with improving your communication skills, in particular those relevant to your creative media production studies. Communication techniques are an essential skill in the creative and media sector, and verbal communication is used all the time, particularly to put across or pitch ideas to clients and colleagues.

You will also be required to produce written documentation, especially in relation to your production work where you will be required to provide paperwork to cover all areas of professional practice (for example, scripts and storyboards). You may also be required to write assignments that reflect your knowledge and understanding of specific subject areas and learning outcomes.

Throughout this course, you will be looking at current practices and applying them to your studies. This means that, at some stage, you will be required to take part in discussions about topics relevant to your chosen optional units. You may find that you will discuss structures and ownership of media industries or take part in relevant debates around reading media texts.

Learning outcomes

After completing this unit you should:

1. be able to communicate about media production in discussions
2. be able to present information and ideas orally to an audience
3. be able to communicate information and ideas in written formats for media production.

Assessment and grading criteria

This table shows you what you must do in order to achieve a **pass**, **merit** or **distinction** grade, and where you can find activities in this book to help you.

To achieve a **pass** grade the evidence must show that you are able to:	To achieve a **merit** grade the evidence must show that, in addition to the pass criteria, you are able to:	To achieve a **distinction** grade the evidence must show that, in addition to the pass and merit criteria, you are able to:
P1 communicate information and ideas in discussions about media production with sufficient clarity to be understood **See Assessment activity 2.1, page 36**	**M1** communicate information and ideas in discussions about media production for the most part clearly **See Assessment activity 2.1, page 36**	**D1** communicate information and ideas in discussions about media production confidently and with consistent clarity **See Assessment activity 2.1, page 36**
P2 use software to create basic presentations **See Assessment activity 2.2, page 43**	**M2** use software to create competent presentations **See Assessment activity 2.2, page 43**	**D2** use software to create effective, well-structured presentations **See Assessment activity 2.2, page 43**
P3 address and interact with an audience appropriately **See Assessment activity 2.2, page 43**	**M3** address and interact with an audience effectively **See Assessment activity 2.2, page 43**	**D3** address and interact with an audience confidently **See Assessment activity 2.2, page 43**
P4 present information and ideas for media production appropriately in written formats with sufficient clarity to be understood **See Assessment activity 2.3, page 50**	**M4** present information and ideas for media production in written formats concisely and for the most part clearly **See Assessment activity 2.3, page 50**	**D4** present information and ideas for media production in written formats clearly with consistent clarity **See Assessment activity 2.3, page 50**
P5 correct documents using basic electronic aids **See Assessment activity 2.3, page 50**	**M5** correct misspellings in documents through effective proofreading **See Assessment activity 2.3, page 50**	**D5** improve clarity of documents through effective proofreading **See Assessment activity 2.3, page 50**

How you will be assessed

Assessment for this unit can take many forms, from assignments requiring written reports or documentation to observed oral presentations and discussions. It is very likely that the work required for this unit will be undertaken in other units, such as video or audio production, and that your tutor will track your progress in an integrated assignment, rather than by separate assessment. Work submitted may be subject to sampling by your centre's External Verifier as part of Edexcel's ongoing quality assurance procedures.

Your assessments could be in the form of:

- written assignments
- pitches to your tutor and classmates
- presentations
- group discussions.

Elaine, Video production

I am quite a shy person and so I chose video production because I could be behind the camera rather than in front of it.

At first, I felt nervous about presenting my ideas for an audience. I was worried they would think my ideas were silly or I wouldn't be able to speak loudly enough. I soon realised the rest of my class felt the same way and that helped me to relax.

I found it helpful to plan carefully what I was going to say. I wrote notes on prompt cards that related to key points and printed out handouts so the audience had something to look through as I talked. This helped take the pressure off me a bit, as they weren't looking at me all the time.

By using the PowerPoint® presentation graphics program, I was able to add in written information as well as charts and animations. This made the presentation more interactive and allowed me to really put my point across.

I did well in the end: everyone liked my ideas and I was pleased with the final product. I think doing presentations has helped build my confidence in all areas. I have found it helpful in group work, because I am more able to put my ideas forward. It has also helped me work as a director during my productions, rather than hiding behind the camera all the time.

- Have you done class presentations before?
- Do you regularly check through your work to make sure it is accurate?
- How do you think good communication skills will help you in the creative media sector?

1. Be able to communicate about media production in discussions

Set up

Plan a discussion

A class discussion can often be a daunting prospect and, having just met a new group of people, you may not feel ready to talk to a large group about the subjects you are studying BTEC Level 2 First Creative Media Production.

Before you take on something you may not be comfortable with, it might be beneficial to discuss ideas and opinions with a smaller group of people with whom you feel more comfortable – maybe friends you have known for a long time or members of your family.

It is also a good idea to choose a topic that you are familiar with and which you already have opinions about: this will allow you to come up with some sound arguments in order to put your point across. Consider what point you are trying to make so that you know what the focus of your argument is.

Participating in group and class discussions is an essential part of your course. You need to be able to talk clearly and thoughtfully about the chosen discussion topic and to interact with your classmates and tutors. There are two main factors to keep in mind during a discussion:

- oral communication skills
- your ability to interact with others.

Case study: Production meetings

In the advertising industry, it is important to hold planning meetings to ensure that everybody knows what the ideas and concepts for the proposed campaign are and how you intend to portray the product to the target audience.

Neil Kulkarni, a music journalist, describes a production meeting in his company:

'Once planning and ideas have been generated and sketched out, we then discuss how effective they will be and how they can best be interpreted on screen, radio or in print. All production team members will have their say and put forward their ideas so we can come up with a final pitch for our clients.

Preparation for these meetings is essential. I expect all members of my team to come to the table knowing where we are with the idea and with plans for how we can move it forward to the next stage.'

- What members of staff are likely to be present at a production meeting in the advertising industry?
- What sort of preparation will you need to do for your production meetings?
- Write a checklist detailing good speaking and listening skills for your group to follow in meetings.

The point of class and group discussions is to allow people to air their views and opinions on certain topics and to assess the relevance of those opinions to your studies. When working on a production, you will need to have discussions with your group in order to generate and form ideas that are relevant and workable. Similarly, in a classroom situation, these discussions will help you to develop your knowledge and understanding of the different topics you are studying; you can then apply this knowledge and understanding to your assignment work.

Why is it important to prepare for any meetings or discussions in which you will be involved?

Activity: Taking part in a discussion

1. Pick a topic that you are comfortable with and outline the points that you want to discuss. Make a plan for yourself and write down your main arguments for your particular viewpoint.

2. Arrange for a group of friends or family members to join in your discussion. Tell them what the topic is and allow them some time to consider their opinions on it beforehand.

3. During the discussion, take note of what has been said by others, and whether or not they agreed with you, so that you can review these points later.

   o How well do you feel the discussion went?

   o Were you confident and able to put across your opinion?

   o Did you change your mind as a result of the discussion or did your opinion stay the same?

Oral communication

Effective oral communication skills are essential to anybody wishing to work in the creative media sector. Whether you are communicating with colleagues on a general, day-to-day basis or working on a wider range of tasks, you will need to make yourself clear at all times to avoid confusing others.

Here are some key points to remember in any discussion, which will ensure that you are clearly understood by others at all times:

- clarity of voice
- tone of voice
- clarity of expression
- use of technical language.

Being able to communicate your ideas clearly is very important when working in the media industry. What do you think you will find most challenging about this aspect of your course?

Clarity of voice

This relates to the way in which you pitch your voice in order to be heard.

If you are too quiet and unassertive in the way that you speak, then others are unlikely to hear what you have to say. This will result in having to repeat what you have said, which may make you seem uncertain of yourself.

Similarly, if you go too far in the opposite direction and talk too loudly, you may come across as domineering or even aggressive. This may put people's backs up and could cause them to feel hostile towards your point of view.

Tone of voice

Tone of voice is different to clarity of voice in that it relates more to the intonation that you use when you speak. We all know that people will be more receptive to somebody who speaks in a reasonable, calm manner than to someone who is slightly sarcastic or who is talking down to us and making us feel belittled or stupid. Be sure to consider your audience and the way that you want them to respond to your point of view.

Clarity of expression

This does not mean the look you have on your face when you are talking, although that is also important. Instead, clarity of expression relates to your ability to speak fluently about your chosen subject. It is difficult to follow someone if they keep saying 'um' or 'er' and never really get to the point; these habits can cause the listener to become bored or uninterested in what you are saying. Your listeners could switch off and stop listening and then you have failed to communicate to them effectively.

Common words and sentences such as 'like' or 'do you know what I mean?' should also be avoided, as they give the impression that the speaker:

- does not have a well-rounded argument
- is not sure of their point
- is almost willing someone to understand them.

Use of technical language

Technical language is extremely relevant to production work. You will be learning a lot of new vocabulary during BTEC Level 2 First Creative Media Production, and you will need to be able to use it comfortably and in the right context.

Interacting with others

It may seem obvious that when you are participating in a discussion you will be interacting with others. However, the way in which you do this is very important and will affect how your ideas are received just as much as the points already outlined above.

You should consider the ideas of others throughout all discussions and make the speaker feel comfortable by being attentive, and respecting their turn to speak. Your body language and facial expressions are also important, because they can tell other people a lot about you and how you feel about what they are saying.

Interacting with others is a part of our everyday life, and we use facial expressions and body language as a means of expressing how we feel, whether intentionally or not.

Remember

Keep in mind the points made in the set up activity, about being prepared before a discussion and making sure you have outlined your ideas before you start. This will allow you to take part confidently and convey your ideas with clarity.

Think about it

Social interaction is an important part of our daily lives. Think about how the communication skills you learn in this unit can be used in your everyday conversations with others.

The way we behave with people we are familiar with will be different from the way we behave with people we have recently met. For instance, when chatting with friends we will often all speak at once, talk over each other and generally use lively and vibrant body language. In contrast, when meeting people for the first time, we are often quite guarded and may keep to ourselves until we assess the situation and feel more comfortable. This is just human nature.

You may find it helpful to observe others and the way that they interact with each other. 'People watching' is a fascinating thing to do, and by observing the facial expressions and body language of others we can often judge how they are feeling in any given situation.

Body language can be a powerful method of non-verbal communication. How can you tell what these people are feeling, just by looking at them?

Activity: Non-verbal communication

Start to take note of the ways in which other people interact and how they express themselves, especially in your own peer group (your classmates) and among your friends and family.

- What differences are there between these social groups?
- Can you tell whether someone is interested or bored by assessing the way they look and their body language?
- Try thinking more about your own actions when you are around others; how expressive are you?
- How do you think your facial expressions and body language make you seem to others?

As mentioned above, these forms of interaction between people are very telling and can say a lot about the way that we feel. When taking part in group discussions, as at any other time, be sure to treat others with respect and show them the consideration you would like them to show you.

When someone is speaking, don't turn away from them or start chatting to the person sat next to you, and avoid the temptation to interrupt them or talk over them, even if you feel that what you have to say is important. The key to a good discussion, whether in a small or large group, is to ensure that everybody has their say and that each person feels that their opinion is valued and given fair consideration.

Remember

When taking part in a discussion, make a note of the points other people are putting forward. Refer back to these points when you are putting your own ideas across.

It is important to treat others with consideration and respect, even if you disagree with what they have to say. How can you make sure that everyone has the chance to contribute to a discussion?

PLTS

Presenting ideas orally, inviting feedback and dealing positively with praise, setbacks and criticism will help you become a more **reflective learner.**

Functional skills

Making valid contributions to class discussions and focus groups will help you develop your **English** skills.

BTEC Assessment activity 2.1 **P1** **M1** **D1**

When addressing this learning outcome you will be required to take part in group discussions, either with the entire class or in smaller groups, as part of your production work. The work for this unit will be assessed in an integrated way, meaning that it will be done as part of your work in other units.

You have been asked to generate ideas for an advertising campaign for a new MP3 player. You will be using an audio-visual medium and will be aiming at a target audience of 13+.

- Take part in a production meeting to discuss ideas for the advertising campaign. Be sure to contribute your own ideas in a way that other team members can understand. **P1**

- Think about what you are going to say and prepare a few ideas ahead of the meeting. **M1**

- Carefully plan what you want to say in the meeting and make sure the ideas that you bring to the table are realistic and appropriate. Thorough preparation will help you to put your points across clearly and confidently. **D1**

Grading tips

To aim for a **merit** grade, you will need to ensure that you have planned what you are going to say and prepared some ideas to contribute that will allow you to make your ideas and opinions clear to others at most times.

To aim for a **distinction** grade, you will need to have carefully planned what you are going to say and prepared some sound and realistic production ideas that will allow you to clearly and confidently take part in the discussion.

2. Be able to present information and ideas orally to an audience

Presentations are an important part of your work for the BTEC Level 2 First Creative Media Production, as they reflect current practice within the industries you will study. It is common for clients who have commissioned a product to require both written and oral presentations of information; these will often take the form of a **pitch** in which you will outline your ideas for the proposed product.

In this section, you will look at the different types of technology that you may be required to use when making a presentation, and the different techniques you can use to communicate with and engage your audience.

Case study: Presentations

Music journalist Neil Kulkarni describes his attitude to presenting himself:

'I've appeared on various panels at industry conventions/label-conventions but really, every interview I've ever done is a kind of presentation. You have to be informed and prepared, with your materials and recording-tech ready, and you need to know your subject inside out and be able to speak to a room full of strangers (only some of whom may be in the band you're interviewing) for a sustained period until you get what you want.'

- How confident are you in public speaking?
- How can you prepare to make sure that you give an effective presentation?
- How will you start and end your presentation?

Copyright issues

Copyright is an important issue to be considered during your production planning. Make sure that the ideas you are presenting are your own and avoid mimicking too closely any that already exist in the creative media sector. You will also need to check that you have permission to use any other sourced materials, such as music scores or photographs. For further information on copyright restrictions, see chapter 4 (Unit 4), Media audiences and products, page 93.

When presenting ideas of a factual nature, take care to get your facts straight, as the following case study will illustrate.

Key term

Pitch – a presentation in which you try to sell your idea for a media production to a potential client.

Case study: Getting your facts right!

As a music journalist, Neil Kulkarni knows the importance of checking the facts in any work you produce:

'Fans are the greatest fact-checkers on earth. If you go to see a band and get so much as one song title wrong in your live review, you'll get a sackload of mail from fans all over the world, calling for your dismissal. Lyrics, song titles, band members' names – you can't get them wrong or it's your head on the block. Thus, painstaking accuracy is something that every journalist should be interested in at all times. The two times I've been sued by a celebrity, both cases ended in a hasty retreat by the celebrity's lawyers when they realised I had my work backed up with tapes and accurate transcripts, and that I had stayed well within the terms of the laws on libel and defamation. No one should start churning out copy without checking the rules first.'

- Why is accuracy so important?
- What can happen if a writer has misrepresented somebody?
- What are the two legal considerations mentioned and what do they mean?

Activity: Presenting your ideas

Presentations probably seem to be one of the most daunting ways in which to put across information and ideas – the thought of giving a presentation can unnerve even the most outgoing people – but they are one of the most effective ways of providing a group of people with ideas and information. For instance, your tutors are presenting their ideas to learners of all ages and backgrounds, every day!

The classroom is a good place for you to start thinking about this learning outcome and will allow you a greater insight into the best ways to present your ideas. When you are in lessons, make a note of the different methods your tutor uses to pass information on to you.

- What different kinds of materials are used in the class, such as handouts and interactive whiteboards?
- How does your tutor use their voice to engage their audience?
- Is their body language also important?

Use your notes to inform your own ideas about how best to conduct a presentation and how to behave in front of an audience.

Had you realised that you have been observing presentations every day when you are at school or college?

Presentation technology

Presentation technology can come in many different formats. It can be as simple as a printed handout to be used as a **visual aid** for your audience, to a more complex presentation produced in PowerPoint®, with imported clips, animations and **transitions**. Transitions are often found in different software packages and add a flourish to your presentation when moving from one screen to the next. Be careful to keep them relevant – don't just add them for effect, as they can become tiresome.

There are many different types of technology available for you to use in your presentations, including PowerPoint®, Keynote application program, Google Docs™ program, SlideRocket and Adobe® Acrobat® software. All of these can help give your presentation style and flair, but remember to consider audience, message and accessibility issues, and keep a balance.

The most important thing to remember about using different **production software** and technologies in your presentations is that they are supposed to aid the audience's understanding. If they are too flashy or complicated, they may distract from the point you are trying to make; if they are dull and uninteresting, they will not appeal to your audience.

When deciding what technology will best suit your purposes, try to consider:

* your audience

* your message

* accessibility issues.

Audience

Who is the audience for your presentation? The age and gender of your audience will factor quite highly in your decisions. Younger generations tend to be highly visual and will enjoy something flashy and eye-catching. An older audience will also enjoy a lively presentation, but be careful that it is not all style and no substance.

> ## Key terms
>
> **Visual aid** – a device used to make your presentation more visually appealing, for example handouts, clipart, video clips, charts, graphs and screen shots.
>
> **Transitions** (presentations) – devices used to add a flourish to a presentation when moving from one slide/screen to the next.
>
> **Production software** – software used to create a presentation.

Audience research

■ What are the interests of your audience?

■ What other products does your audience consume?

■ Are you targeting one gender or both?

■ What age group is your product targeted at?

Figure 2.1: These examples of presentation slides contain the same information, but it has been presented in different ways. Think about how you can vary the style and format of your presentations so they are appropriate for your intended audience.

Message

What do you want to say in your presentation? It is important to focus on the main points that you want to make and then try to highlight them with some clever or carefully chosen images. Too much text can clutter the page and may be hard for the audience to focus on. Go too far the other way and they will be too busy looking at your clever artwork to concentrate on you and what you are saying.

Accessibility

Where will your presentation take place? This may seem obvious, but it has been the downfall of many a presentation in the past. There is no point in planning a wonderful, all-singing, all-dancing, interactive presentation for a room that doesn't have the facility to project it to the audience.

Consider how your audience will be seated during the presentation. Will they have an unobstructed, direct view of your presentation? If the layout of the room means that some of the audience don't have a good view, your first consideration should be changing this layout. If that is not possible, think about other means of allowing them full access to your presentation, such as a colourful or illustrated handout.

Interacting with the audience

This is where the information and techniques you have learned earlier in your discussions will come in helpful. You will now need to expand on these skills in order to engage a different audience; this time you will have to do all the talking and may need to answer questions at the end.

Structure your presentation so that it has:

- a beginning (or **introduction**)
- a middle, which will be the part where you present your information
- an end (or **conclusion**), where you summarise your point.

There are plenty of tips and pointers for you to follow that are not only important but essential to ensure a successful presentation.

Try to ensure **clarity of voice** throughout your presentation using the correct **style, tone** and **register**. For example, be calm and in control for the most part, but also try to inject some humour to keep the audience at ease.

Be sure to use appropriate **technical** and **vocational** language where necessary, and **maintain engagement** throughout by using good **eye contact** and **referencing points** in handouts and on the screen.

Remember

Always try to produce a handout for the audience that will help them to follow what is being said. Remember to allow them a little time to read it **before** starting your presentation.

Preparation

If you are at the stage where you are ready to make a presentation then you have already made use of the relevant technology and compiled a presentation that you think will work effectively.

Once you have all the necessary information in your presentation and you are happy with the layout, it is advisable to write a script for yourself in order to practise what you are going to say. Use this script to rehearse as often as possible beforehand, so that you are clear on what you want to say and you can start to focus on your delivery.

Activity: The dress rehearsal

Any activity is easier to undertake once you have practised it a few times. Like learning to ride or any other new skill – and presenting is a skill – the more you do it the better you will get. Actors rehearse their lines before they appear in front of an audience and there is no reason why you shouldn't do the same!

1. First make sure that you have your script or cue cards written up in legible writing and in a format that you are comfortable with.

2. Next spend some time familiarising yourself with what you are going to say. Read through your script a few times so that you have a clear idea of what you are going to say.

3. Now it's time to practise saying it all out loud. You can do this in a number of ways, but the best ones are:

   o Practise in front of the mirror. You are less likely to feel self conscious and it will give you a chance to see what everyone else is going to see.

   o Present to a friend or your family. They are the people most likely to oblige and you can be guaranteed of honest feedback.

Once you have rehearsed a couple of times, you can reflect on how you have done, maybe even respond to the feedback if you gained any, and make any necessary changes as a result.

The presentation

Engaging your audience is probably the biggest issue facing any presenter, but if you have prepared carefully and rehearsed well this will help boost your confidence and make you more relaxed and confident.

Make eye contact

Remember to focus on your audience and make eye contact with them at all times. That's not to say you can't sometimes look at the screen behind you or refer to your cue cards, but you should look your audience in the eye when you are addressing them; be sure to include each member of the audience with this eye contact.

Use your voice

Speak clearly and project your voice so that everyone can hear you (but don't shout). Your voice is the most powerful tool to use in presentations and the pitch and tone of it can really make a difference. You can put emphasis on words and sentences to stress their importance or you can be light hearted and conversational to put your audience at ease and make them warm to you.

The intention of your presentation is to get your audience on your side and thinking about your ideas; the best way to do this is to engage them on a personal level. Be funny but don't act the clown; take charge but try not to be overpowering, and make sure that you maintain your audience's interest by providing information in the most interesting way possible.

Body language

Use open and positive body language. This means you should open your hands out and look relaxed and at ease, maybe move about a bit instead of being static and rigid. Always face your audience, avoid turning your back on them and make sure you arrange yourself so that it should never be necessary to do so.

The end

Bring your presentation to a reasonable conclusion that the audience can follow (don't just finish abruptly). It can be helpful to say something like **'so in conclusion'** before you make your final point and be sure to thank audience members for their time. It is also advisable to invite questions to allow the audience to clarify any points they might not have been able to follow.

Acting and presenting use many of the same skills. How many similarities can you think of?

Assessment activity 2.2

For this learning outcome, you are assessed on your ability to take part in presentations, using appropriate formats, and on your interaction with your audience.

You have used the discussion in Assessment activity 2.1 to plan ideas for the MP3 player advert; you now need to present those ideas to your client.

Create a presentation, using appropriate formats, that outlines your ideas and suggestions to your client. Be sure to add visuals to help make your point.

- Use software to create a basic presentation, including slides, and containing verbal information. Be sure to address and interact with your audience appropriately. **P2 P3**

- Prepare written information for your audience to read and include graphics to illustrate what you are saying. Do a practice run of your presentation to make sure you know how the software works. Try to control your pitch and tone as you speak, and maintain eye contact with your audience. **M2 M3**

- Rehearse your presentation in front of a friend and ask for feedback so that you can make revisions to its structure and improve its effectiveness. Make sure that any graphics you use are relevant to the points you make. Speak with confidence when you interact with your audience. **D2 D3**

Grading tips

To aim for a **merit** grade, you need to provide a presentation that has been competently produced using relevant software. You need to effectively communicate with your audience throughout using good pitch and tone and maintaining eye contact for most of the time.

To aim for a **distinction** grade, you need to provide a well-structured presentation that includes relevant and targeted information that effectively illustrates your point. You must show confidence when interacting with your audience, maintaining eye contact and clarity throughout.

PLTS

Communicating information and ideas in relevant ways for different audiences using oral presentations and written formats will help you become a more **reflective learner**.

Functional skills

Checking and evaluating information used in charts and graphs will help you to develop your **Mathematics** skills.

3. Be able to communicate information and ideas in written formats for media production

The final section of this unit is concerned with your written communication skills. Throughout your studies, you will be asked to produce written documents in many different formats, such as:

- essays
- assignments
- production paperwork, such as scripts, storyboards, pitches and **treatments**.

You need to make sure that all of these documents are fit for purpose and free from errors by using skills such as proofreading and spell checking; this will also help you to improve your English skills.

Key term

Treatment – the initial outline of your proposed production, providing details of scenes, characters and locations.

Activity: Examples of texts

Here are some examples of the different formats of text that you may come into contact with during your studies.

Proposal

PRODUCTION OUTLINE:
To produce a lively, colourful and vibrant advertisement for a new mid-price MP3 player that is due to be launched. This is an audio-visual advertisement that will have images of young people similar to those found in the target audience; they will be listening to music on their MP3 players and doing everyday things that the audience can relate to.

PRODUCTION PURPOSE:
To launch a new product onto the market, to entice the consumer and to raise brand awareness.

TARGET AUDIENCE:
Teenagers aged 14–18 who like to listen to music but cannot afford the more expensive MP3 players that are available on the market.

Sound/Music
Cast: Three teenagers, one male, two female aged 16–18.
Storyline: Glimpses of target audience's everyday life showing them consuming the product so that they can relate to it.
Locations: External locations, on the street, in college, on the bus and walking through the park.

Figure 2.2: A sample proposal for a media production. Why is it important to ensure that all pre-production paperwork is clear and up to date?

3. MUSIC:	DANGER THEME – ESTABLISH – FADE UNDER.
4* JOHNNY-BOY:	Look out! They've thrown a refrigerator out the window!
5. SOUND:	REFRIGERATOR CRASH. WALLA-SCREAMS.
6* SUZANNE:	(GASP) Oh no! Johnny-Boy's flatter than a pancake!
7. NARRATOR:	(SIGH) Sadly, Johnny-Boy wound up just one more ghost. Meanwhile, Kitty had to deal with ghosts of a different sort.

*Asterisks beside the cue numbers in the script alert the director, cast and crew that they must pay attention to delivering this cue at a timing determined by the director.

Figure 2.3: A sample radio script, marked up for the FX team. How has the scriptwriter used music and sound effects to enhance the action in this piece? Source: http://ruyasonic. com/prd_pre-prod.htm

1. Try to identify where and when each type of document may be used.

2. Try filling out at least one of these documents by hand. Once you have done this, check through your work for errors without using spell-checking software to help you.

3. Assess how well you have done by asking someone else to review your work and feedback to you.

4. How thorough were your checks? Did you find any or all of the errors you made? How hard did you find this activity without the use of relevant software?

Production schedule

Day	Work to be done	By whom	By when
1	Planning meeting to discuss ideas for factual video product	All group members	Add date
2	Second planning meeting to review and finalise ideas	All group members	
3	Work on planning documents, scripts, storyboards, risk assessments	Group members assigned individual roles	
4	Work on planning documents, scripts, storyboards, risk assessments	Group members assigned individual roles	
5	Shoot footage on locations, scenes 1, 3 and 5	Director, camera operator and cast	
6	Shoot footage on locations, scenes 4, 7 and 10	Director, camera operator and cast	
7	Edit footage adding transitions, sound effects, music and titles	Editor	
8	Edit footage adding transitions, sound effects, music and titles	Editor	
9	Review final edit	All group members	

Figure 2.4: This is an example of a production schedule and how it could be filled in. What other information might you need to add when planning your own production?

Formats

There are many different formats your work will take. For example, in video production you will need to prepare proposals or treatments, as well as other **production documentation** such as scripts and storyboards. Production documentation covers all production paperwork from pre-production to post-production. All industry sectors have their own different sets of required paperwork to help ensure the production process runs smoothly. All the documentation requires a written as well as a creative element. You will need to fill out some of this paperwork by hand and will not always be able to rely on computer software to do the work for you.

Reports and essays will also be required, especially in theoretical units such as Units 1, 3 and 4; these will allow you to present information to your tutor and enables them to assess your understanding of the topics you have covered in class.

When conducting research, you may find that you need to contact companies and individuals to ask them to provide information for you (primary research). You can do this by sending emails outlining your requirements; this is often one of the quickest ways of getting a response.

Another area you may consider is group work, as often this requires organising a number of people and making sure they all do their required jobs at the right time. You may have to record the **minutes** of meetings, create and give out schedules, or produce **memos** as a reminder to others of what is going on in your productions. Memos are a very useful organisational tool.

Key terms

Production documentation – documentation covering all production paperwork from pre-production to post-production.

Minutes – a written summary of who was at a meeting, what was said and what actions were agreed.

Memo – short for 'memorandum', a memo is a brief note with details of things to be done or remembered.

Date: Time: Place:

Present:

Apologies: Minutes taken by:

Minutes

Figure 2.5: This is an example of a **meeting record sheet**. Why is it important to record this information during meetings?

Shot: Framing:	Shot: Framing:	Shot: Framing:
Duration:____ Shot size:___ Angle:___ Transition:___ Audio 1:___ Audio 2:___	Duration:____ Shot size:___ Angle:___ Transition:___ Audio 1:___ Audio 2:___	Duration:____ Shot size:___ Angle:___ Transition:___ Audio 1:___ Audio 2:___
Shot: Framing:	Shot: Framing:	Shot: Framing:
Duration:____ Shot size:___ Angle:___ Transition:___ Audio 1:___ Audio 2:___	Duration:____ Shot size:___ Angle:___ Transition:___ Audio 1:___ Audio 2:___	Duration:____ Shot size:___ Angle:___ Transition:___ Audio 1:___ Audio 2:___

Figure 2.6: This is a sample **storyboard** for a media production. Will you be able to fill in a storyboard like this for one of your productions?

Activity: Structuring an essay

When writing an essay it is important to get the structure and order right so that it is easy to read, ensuring that you consistently keep to your theme or point and draw your work to a reasonable conclusion.

The tips outlined here should give you some guidance on how best to do this.

1. Identify the topic.

2. Come up with some ideas on how best to tackle the subject area.

3. Conduct some research to provide you with the information you need to make up your content.

4. When you begin writing, start by outlining your ideas/thoughts/purpose.

5. Next, provide an introduction to outline your topic and give a clear indication of what the essay will be about.

6. The main body of the essay is where you look in detail at the topic you are writing about, providing information, ideas, arguments and quotes for reference.

7. Write a conclusion to your topic or argument that states your position and summarises what you have already discussed.

8. Finally comes the editing and proofreading stage to ensure your work is free from errors.

Use this activity the next time you get an assignment and see if it improves the layout of your work.

Vocabulary

Although this may seem like an area that is linked to oral work or presentations, **vocabulary** is also important in your written work. For the most part, your written work should use either technical or formal vocabulary or a mixture of both. This is because the main body of your written work will be assignments and essays or production paperwork that requires you to use these types of vocabulary.

There will be very few occasions when you will need to use informal language as this is not relevant to your work, although it may be that memos or emails to friends about group meetings may fall into a less formal pattern of writing. It is best, however, to try to remain professional at all times. Steer clear of using informal language in essay and assignment work, and avoid being chatty or using slang at all times.

Remember

You should always consider your audience when undertaking written work. Keep in mind what you want to say and how you want it to be received by your audience. Use language appropriately and in the right context, otherwise it won't make sense.

Activity: Appropriate vocabulary

Below are extracts from two essays written by First Diploma learners. One of them has used appropriate vocabulary and the other has used a more informal style of language. Can you identify which is which and, if so, how? Make a note of the main differences in terms of use of vocabulary.

Example 1

The technical skills needed in order to become an animator are firstly being able to draw 2-D or 3-D drawings by hand. You also need to be able to make slight adjustments to 3-D models to create a moving sequence and draw 2-D or 3-D drawings on computer. You will also need to have some modelling skills, be computer literate and familiar with graphics software including Adobe® Photoshop® and Flash®.

In terms of personal skills, creativity and imagination are extremely important as are patience and attention to detail. The ability to meet deadlines and the ability to work well as part of a team are essential.

Overall, you will need to have more technical than personal skills. This is a job for a person who knows where they are going and can get on with it.

Example 2

For the first assignment, I did some research about the guide to the media industry. On this assignment, I looked at different things about media and I used one particular website that was very useful www.wikipedia.org.

The second assignment is about media audiences. On this assignment I got all my research on this certain website www.barb.co.uk it was very useful because I got all the information I needed to know about the media audiences. I also used the website www.wikipedia.org for the regulations.

Now make a note of where technical language is being used within these texts. Which individual words or sentences give these extracts a formal, rather than an informal, feel?

Discuss these extracts within your group and see if you can suggest ways that they could be improved. Can they be made more interesting but still maintain their formal content?

Revision

Checking through your work and ensuring that it is fit for purpose and ready to be submitted for assessment is essential. You might have made some errors or omissions in your work; these can change the whole meaning of sentences, which will result in you not putting your point across properly.

The following list provides some key points to remember.

- First, check the **structure of your content.** Does it make sense? Is everything in the right order? Have you followed the guidelines outlined above and made sure there is a beginning, middle and end?

- **Clarity of expression** relates to how well you have made your point and in what way. Have you used the right expression, pitch and phrases? Is it clear what you have written? There has to be consistency in the use of language, grammar, spelling and meaning.

- Carry out **electronic checks** on your spelling, punctuation and grammar to ensure they are correct. Most word-processing packages for the Mac computer and PC will have this facility. You should use these on a regular basis, but only as a first-line check on your work.

- **Proofreading** is then essential. You will have to do this individually and without using technology. You need to read through your work carefully and check for any errors that may be left after the initial spell check has been done. Remember that a spell check only checks the spelling of a word, not the context; so if you put 'their' instead of 'there', or vice versa, it may not tell you!

Activity: Proofreading

Here is an extract from a learner's assignment. Some of the content is incorrect, the spelling and grammar is not completely correct and it is evident that this work, although it may have been spell checked, has not been proofread.

Read through the extract and highlight the errors.

How many spelling errors are there?

How many grammatical errors are there?

Try rewriting this extract and see if you could put it in a better order with fewer errors. Remember the word processor isn't always your friend and a miskey may not always be picked up by a spell checker.

The young ones hove used equilibrium by having their normal life in the flat then disrupting their life this is called disequilibrium for example when Vyvyan smashes through the wall in the episode called 'demolition' because their house is going to be demolished because they haven't paid the bells and when they come to demolish the house Rick has attached himself to a cross on the font of the house, this shows his childish behaviour because it is a immature thing to do, Neil is running around outside the front of the house with a pot of lintels then Vyvyan knocks a hole in the side of the house.

I feel that the target audience would be people in their late teens and early twenties as the cast are playing students and use language they would understand.

A lot of young people at the time weren't hoppy with the way Margret Thatcher was running the country as their were a lot of strikes and the Young Ones dealt with this in a humus way, with Rick who was partly this political arteries part childlike character who is obsessed with Cliff Richard and bed poetry and how bad Margaret Thatcher is or as he calls her 'Maggie'.

Assessment activity 2.3

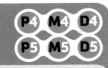

For this learning outcome, you need to focus on accuracy and presenting work in the correct format that is free from errors. You need to use your own skills as well as current software packages to check through your work, ensuring it is fit for purpose and free of errors.

Your ideas for the MP3 player advert have been accepted by the client and now you have to start the pre-production phase of your production. Use documentation and formats relevant to the audio-visual medium you will be working in, so scripts, storyboards and production schedules will be essential. You should also produce minutes of all planning meetings.

- Present your ideas and supporting information using relevant documentation and formats for audio-visual production. Correct your documents using basic electronic aids, such as a computer spell checker. **P4** **P5**

- Proofread your documentation to check for errors in spelling, punctuation and grammar, and to make sure it makes sense. **M4** **M5**

- Check that all of your documentation is concise and of a consistently high standard. It should be error free, following regular proofreading. **D4** **D5**

Grading tips

To aim for a **merit** grade, you need to be able to produce work of a good standard, making sound use of relevant documentation and formats. You must use your own skills rather than electronic aids to carry out your spell checks by proofreading your work.

To aim for a **distinction** grade, you need to be able to produce work of a consistent standard, making concise use of relevant documentation and formats. You must be consistent in the accuracy of your work, showing that you regularly and correctly proofread your work to check for errors.

PLTS

Presenting written information using reasoned arguments and evidence, and providing supporting evidence, will help you to develop your skills as an **independent enquirer**.

Functional skills

Gathering and annotating research from a variety of sources, and proofreading and spell checking documents before submission, will help you to improve your **English** skills.

Neil Kulkarni
Music journalist

In 1994, I was fresh out of uni when I wrote a letter to my favourite music magazine about what I thought they were doing wrong. It was printed and the editor responded, saying 'do you think you can do any better?' I wrote back to say 'yeah, I do actually' and was commissioned to do some sample articles.

As my writing got seen by other editors I got used more. Soon my life became a whirlwind of gigs, interviews and international trips, but as a freelancer with no training I was struggling to manage my time, travel, finances and workflow.

Spelling and grammar can now be checked by computer, but when I started out all work was typed and faxed. That gave me a good grounding in not just trusting word-processing programs! You have to **read** something before you submit it, because hearing the words out loud and seeing them in print reveals mistakes that computer programs simply don't see.

Throughout the writing process, being good at spelling and grammar makes your writing easier and more fluid, and shows your editors that you care about your work. No matter how fast you may have to create copy, checking it before you submit it is crucial. The process that goes on in my area of the industry is this:

1. Writer pitches idea.

2. Editor either rejects idea or approves it and gives you a wordcount and deadline.

3. You submit your piece on time, within the wordcount, with any extra images/interviews attached. If you haven't checked the grammar and spelling, or you miss deadlines, it puts an extra burden on the sub-editors at the magazine. Simply put, they will stop using you.

Think about it

1. List some of the most important things that Neil mentions in relation to accuracy in his work.

2. How important do you think it is to meet deadlines in the creative media sector?

3. If you are working to a deadline and don't plan correctly, how can that affect the consistency and accuracy of your work?

4. How reliable are word-processing programs as a means of checking your work?

Just checking

1. Outline the three most important things to keep in mind when planning for a discussion.
2. In discussions and presentations, it is important to put across your views and opinions clearly and concisely. Can you remember how to do this?
3. What is non-verbal communication?
4. Name some of the presentation technologies you can use for presenting your ideas.
5. What are animations and how can they enhance your presentation?
6. What formats and documents may you need to use during production planning?
7. What are the four key points to remember during revision of work?
8. What are the three phases of essay writing?
9. What is the difference between technical and formal vocabulary?
10. Why is it important to proofread your work as well as perform an electronic check?

Assignment tips

- Before a discussion, plan what you are going to say and think about any counter arguments that people may bring up so you have a response prepared.
- When planning your presentation try to condense your script into key words or prompts, bullet pointed and written on cue cards. Cue cards are smaller and easier to handle and you can refer to them during the presentation.
- For proofreading, invest in a highlighter pen. Whenever you have finished writing a piece of work, print it out and read through it carefully. Highlight the areas where you have made mistakes and then revisit it to make the necessary corrections.
- When constructing a presentation using PowerPoint®, search for interesting material to include, such as pictures, clips and links. The Internet is a great resource, so use it, but be careful not to breach copyright. Look for images that are copyright-free or for which not all rights are reserved.
- When taking part in discussions, good planning is essential. It is important to be sure of yourself and to put your point across assertively; being well prepared means you are less likely to come across as agitated or aggressive.
- Rehearsing or practising your presentation is vital. You will be assessed on your performance as well as the content of your slideshow, so you need to be calm, clear and concise.

3 The creative media sector

The creative media sector is made up of many different media industries, such as television, film, radio, print and interactive media. All of these industries produce their own distinctive products, often using unique formats and utilising or combining many different genres.

The products produced by these industries are consumed by all of us on a regular basis and often as part of our everyday lives, so it is important to understand how they are structured, as well as how they are run and by whom.

It is likely that you wish to work in one of these industries once you have finished your studies; therefore, this unit also looks at the different job roles and skills required to work within the creative media sector and the way in which you can start looking for work. This can be done by reflecting on skills and qualifications, and looking at ways of improving on them to make yourself more 'marketable', helping you to find that dream job.

Learning outcomes

After completing this unit you should:

1. know how the creative media sector is structured
2. know about job roles and conditions of employment in a creative media industry
3. know how to gain employment in a creative media industry.

Assessment and grading criteria

This table shows you what you must do in order to achieve a **pass**, **merit** or **distinction** grade, and where you can find activities in this book to help you.

To achieve a **pass** grade the evidence must show that you are able to:	To achieve a **merit** grade the evidence must show that, in addition to the pass criteria, you are able to:	To achieve a **distinction** grade the evidence must show that, in addition to the pass and merit criteria, you are able to:
P1 outline the structure of the creative media sector **See Assessment activity 3.1, page 61**	**M1** describe the structure of the creative media sector with some detail and with reference to appropriate illustrative examples **See Assessment activity 3.1, page 61**	**D1** explain the structure of the creative media sector with reference to precise and detailed illustrative examples **See Assessment activity 3.1, page 61**
P2 describe job roles and conditions of employment in a creative media industry **See Assessment activity 3.2, page 69**	**M2** describe job roles and conditions of employment in a creative media industry with some detail and with reference to appropriate illustrative examples **See Assessment activity 3.2, page 69**	**D2** explain job roles and conditions of employment in a creative media industry with reference to precise and detailed illustrative examples **See Assessment activity 3.2, page 69**
P3 describe how to obtain employment in a creative media industry **See Assessment activity 3.3, page 74**	**M3** describe how to obtain employment in a creative media industry with some detail and with reference to appropriate illustrative examples **See Assessment activity 3.3, page 74**	**D3** explain how to obtain employment in a creative media industry with reference to precise and detailed illustrative examples **See Assessment activity 3.3, page 74**

How you will be assessed

Work for this unit is likely to take the form of written assignments that will allow you to express your ideas and understanding, or individual presentations using computer presentation software, both of which are designed to assess your understanding of the creative media sector. This unit will be assessed internally by your tutors. However, all work submitted may be subject to sampling by your centre's External Verifier as part of Edexcel's ongoing quality assurance procedures.

Your assessments could be in the form of:

* written reports
* class presentations
* audio-visual presentations.

Stuart, Audio production

I have always been really interested in music and would love to work in the radio industry as a DJ some day. I know that it isn't going to happen over night and that I have to work hard at it, but that is all I have really wanted to do since I was young.

I feel that, as a result of studying this unit, I know more about what to expect when I finally get a job in the industry. I understand more about contracts of employment and how and what I am likely to get paid for the work that I want to do.

The best thing we did was researching recruitment processes. We investigated things like where to look for jobs and what skills we need for the job we were interested in. We also started to understand the application process and how best to 'sell ourselves' to an employer. I think this information will really help me in the future and I now feel more prepared for the challenges ahead.

This unit has helped me realise that finding work in the creative media sector is something that needs time and consideration. I know now that I am going to have to either get some good grades as a result of this course and carry on with my education or start looking for a voluntary position to gain some experience, maybe even both.

* What challenges do you think lie ahead when looking for work in a creative media industry?
* Are there any skills that you already have that will help you find a job?
* How do you feel this unit will help you to gain a better understanding of the creative media sector?

1. Know how the creative media sector is structured

Set up

Media diary

In our daily lives we are almost always in contact with some form of media product or service; we are surrounded by it throughout the day.

To analyse this, a group of you could keep a media diary for one day. When you get up in the morning, write down the first time you come into contact with a media product from any of the following industries:

- television
- radio
- press
- music
- film
- interactive media
- photography
- advertising.

When it is complete, look through your media diary and match each industry to the products it produces.

The **creative media sector** comprises the media industry as a whole, including all areas of media production, from traditional to interactive media. In order to gain employment in the creative media sector, you first need to gain an understanding of:

- how it is structured (who owns what, how big the sector is and what sort of products it produces)
- what sort of industries make up the creative media sector, such as television, radio and print
- the ways in which these **industry sectors** operate in terms of **structure**.

Whilst it will be important for you to gain an overview of the sector as a whole, it will be beneficial to focus your work on the particular industry that you will be working in, such as television, film or radio.

Key terms

Creative media sector – includes all areas of media production, from traditional to interactive media.

Industry sectors – the different parts of the media industry categorised by their type of output, for example, television, film, radio and print.

Structure – how a company or industry is organised.

What specific skills and interests will help someone to become a successful radio DJ?

Industry sectors

The creative media sector consists of many different industries that produce their own particular products and services that are designed for different purposes.

Television programmes can be educational, informative or entertaining and so can films, books, magazines and radio programmes.

Newer, interactive media industries offer us the ability to search the Web for information and chat with friends via email and live chat; they enable us to connect with people and businesses from all over the world.

The advertising and marketing industries keep us informed of new and existing products being produced by all types of companies, and use persuasive techniques to entice us to buy them.

Who does what?

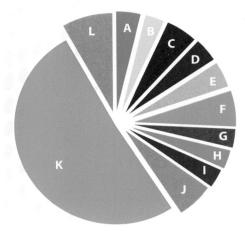

A - Actors and Entertainers 4%
B - Advertising and Public Relations Managers 3%
C - Artists 5%
D - Arts Administrators 4%
E - Authors and Writers 4%
F - Broadcasting Associate Professionals 6%
G - Graphic Designers 3%
H - Journalists 3%
I - Marketing and Sales Managers 3%
J - Musicians 6%
K - Other Occupations 51%
L - Photo and Audio/Visual Operators 8%

Figure 3.1: Market share of jobs in the creative media sector. Source: National Statistics (Nomis). How many jobs can you think of that might fall into the 'Other' category (K)?

Activity: Researching different industries

In a group or pairs, conduct some initial research into the following media industry sectors:

- television and film
- music production and radio
- press and photo imaging
- advertising and marketing
- interactive media.

You can do this by looking at relevant websites such as Skillset or company specific sites such as the BBC. To obtain links to these websites, please see the Hotlinks section on page ii. You can also use some of the textbooks available in your school or college library for your research.

1. Make a note of some of the different companies that operate in these industry sectors and the types of products and services they provide.

2. See if you can find companies that operate within more than one medium.

3. Discuss your findings with the group.

Size, shape and structure of the media sector

Media ownership

How media companies are structured and who owns them is very important as it can have an effect on the types of products and services that they provide. Some companies are huge multinationals with interests in many countries; they may also produce lots of different types of products.

Cross-media

Virgin is an example of a **cross-media producer**; it is a record label that signs bands and artists. This branch of the company will most likely produce music for release on CDs, which is an audio format, but they will also produce music videos – often as a promotional tool – that will be aired on television or sold as DVDs, both of which are audio-visual formats.

As you can see, a company that deals with music production will not restrict their distribution of that music to just one format. This means they are able to reach a wider audience with their products and services and, as a result, make more money. This also means that the company is using **cross-media formats** and more often than not they will distribute their products globally. They may even have subsidiaries in other countries so they can keep an eye out for new up-and-coming artists from around the globe to sign.

Multinational

Rupert Murdoch is the founder and chairman of one of the world's largest **multimedia conglomerates** called News Corporation, which includes British Sky Broadcasting. This company produces books, magazines, newspapers, films, music, radio, television and films, as well as being one of the biggest broadcasters of satellite and cable television.

News International is a **subsidiary** company of News Corporation and operates in the UK. This company owns some of the UK's biggest-selling newspapers, including *The Sun* and *The Times*.

National

The BBC is the oldest broadcasting company in the UK; it began on radio and then moved into television broadcasting on the channel we now know as BBC1. Today it consists of many terrestrial and digital channels, radio stations and an interactive website. Even though the BBC is funded by the television licence, it also makes money from other areas of the creative media sector such as:

- merchandise
- books

Think about it

Who owns and controls the media has a huge effect on how we receive information and in what format. It is important for you to think about and understand where our information is coming from and what the interests are of the people providing it.

- DVDs
- CDs
- magazines
- selling programmes to other companies or networks.

Small scale

Not all companies work on such a large scale and there are still plenty of locally-based media producers that specialise in offering small-scale, more personalised products and services.

Local newspapers and radio stations are common throughout the UK and provide essential news and entertainment. These companies work on a much smaller scale and rely heavily on advertising revenue from local and national companies as a means of generating income.

Some companies also work in marketing and produce leaflets and mailings for large companies to:

- advertise special offers
- provide money-off vouchers
- raise brand awareness.

These smaller companies often work closely with the local community, providing publicity for charity events, traffic reports and essential advertising space to smaller local businesses.

The creative media sector, however, is a very competitive environment. Both large and small companies alike need to be **innovative** and **versatile** in the creation of their products to ensure a steady or growing market for their products.

Many media companies now have their own website. Look at a selection of these and compare the different ways in which the companies are managed and funded.

Assessment activity 3.1 P1 M1 D1

This activity is aimed at helping you to collate the information you have gathered as a result of your research, using it to reflect your understanding of the creative media sector and how it is structured.

Look into the BBC, its structure and its products.

1. On page 59, the BBC is listed as a national company because it is a company owned in Britain. However, do you think there are any reasons why the BBC can be thought of as a multinational company?
2. What is meant by the term 'publicly owned'?
3. What size do you think the BBC is and would you class it as a cross-media producer?
4. The BBC is still strictly known as a public service broadcaster, what do you think this means?

The BBC's website (please see the Hotlinks section on page ii) contains details about its products and services, its history and how it is run. You can use this website to help you find answers to the above questions. As the BBC has been running for many years it has been written about by many people; your library may have some sources of information too.

Once you have looked into the BBC try comparing it to another company, maybe a commercial one such as ITV or Channel 4. See if you can find any similarities or differences.

- Write up your research, outlining the structure of the television industry. **P1**
- Include some detailed examples of how the television industry is structured. **M1**
- Explain and try to evaluate the size, structure and ownership of the television industry. Include precise and detailed examples to illustrate what you are saying. **D1**

Grading tips

To aim for a **merit** grade, you need to do more than just provide a basic outline of the creative media sector. You **must** be sure to use some sound examples from your research that will help you to illustrate your point, ensuring you focus on the size, structure and ownership of your chosen industry.

To aim for a **distinction** grade, you must show a detailed understanding of the creative media sector you have chosen and how it is structured. You must use sound, well thought out examples in order to make your point precisely, explaining the size, structure and ownership of your chosen industry.

Activity: On your doorstep

Investigate a media producer in your local area such as a local newspaper or radio station.

1. Find out how long the company has been operating in your area.
2. How big is the company? Is it a small concern or has it been bought out by a bigger media company?
3. What products or services does the company offer to the local community?
4. Discuss your findings with members of your class. Try to establish how important this company is to your local community.

PLTS

Supporting conclusions in written and oral work, using reasoned arguments and evidence, will help you to develop your skills as an **independent enquirer**.

Functional skills

Sourcing and searching web pages, screen shots and CD-ROMs when conducting research on the creative media sector will help you develop your **ICT** skills.

2. Know about job roles and conditions of employment in a creative media industry

For this learning outcome, you need to look into and understand the different job roles within the creative media industry you are focusing on, and the conditions of employment that you can expect. Consider all possible areas of work that will require you to use different skills and knowledge, from creative and technical positions to managerial and administrative work.

Professional **codes of practice and conduct** are also important. Think about how they affect some of the more creative areas of the industry, where your work may ultimately be consumed by the general public and, as a result, will need to be suitable for its target audience.

Much of the work in the creative media sector is done on a 'flexible' basis. Later in this section, you will learn about the different contracts of employment that are available in the industry.

Key terms

Creative skills – skills required to generate ideas and concepts in order to create media products.

Technical skills – skills and knowledge needed to operate and work with technical equipment such as in a radio studio.

Activity: Personal skills

Look at and reflect upon the jobs that you would like to gain in the industry. Are you interested in working behind the camera in either film or television? Do you have an interest in sound, lighting, editing or props and special effects?

Similarly, you might have a talent for programming and games design, or you might find that operating the equipment in a radio studio is the best way to spend your time and utilise your talents.

There are many jobs in the industry that require people to use different skills and talents. **Creative skills** are the skills required to generate ideas and concepts in order to create media products. They include being artistic or being able to visualise or realise a project. **Technical skills** are the skills and knowledge you need in order to operate and work with technical equipment such as cameras and in editing suites. It is essential to identify your own skills base and ensure that you work hard on developing those relevant to your chosen field.

Think carefully about the type of person you are and the things you enjoy doing. Remember, you will be working for many years so it is important to find a role that you will be happy to work in for the long term.

1. Write a mini personal profile outlining your overall personal attributes, your strengths and your weaknesses.

2. Reflect on your creative and technical skills and outline areas for improvement that you wish to develop.

3. Now try to match the skills that you have at present to the sort of work you would like to do in a creative media industry.

4. Is there a strong match between your skills and the job you want? What can you do to improve the essential skills required for that job?

Job roles

Job roles in the creative media sector can usually be categorised according to the skills required. There are many different levels to any job role. Most people will probably work in a junior or trainee position before progressing to a more senior level as their career progresses.

Below is a description of the different skills areas, as well as a table of job roles matched to their particular area. The table highlights possible jobs available in all industries within the creative media sector and provides a brief outline of the job description.

- **Technical** – this relates to the ability to work with equipment and technology in order to create media products.

- **Creative** – a creative skill can be any skill that lets you expand on what there already is, for example, designing page layouts or creating storyboards. You can continue on an idea and you are not limited in your ability to create.

- **Editorial** – very often found in the print industry, this skill relates to the ability to check through work, review what has been produced and provide suggestions, make alterations or bring the work together into a final piece.

- **Managerial** – the ability to oversee the work of others and to organise your own time effectively and productively. This job role will require excellent communication skills and the ability to work well with others.

- **Sales and marketing** – often a role that requires sound interpersonal skills, sales and marketing jobs are very competitive and require you to effectively communicate with others, as well as the ability to get them to buy your product or service.

- **Financial** – being able to generate revenue is important for all creative media industries and that money needs to be handled carefully, channelled into new projects and accounted for at all times.

Jobs in the creative media sector require a huge range of different skills. What do you consider to be your strengths and weaknesses?

Table 3.1: Job roles available within the creative media industries. Which of these roles is best suited to your strengths and weaknesses?

Job role	Description	Skills area
Web developer	Individuals that develop applications on the World Wide Web, working for all types of company	Technical
Technical producer	Responsible for operating studio equipment that controls the on-air product in a radio station for both national and local broadcasters	Technical
Technical director	An expert in a specific field of a chosen industry, who possesses a high level of competence in their chosen field; can work for software companies, theatres and film and television studios	Technical
Web designer	Responsible for how a website looks and how user-friendly its design is; requires technical skills to produce web content	Creative/technical
Writer	Writes scripts for television, film and radio; can work in many genres and must be able to come up with new and original ideas	Creative
Director	In charge of the aesthetic of a film and directs all of the crew, telling them what to do and when to do it	Creative
Set designer	Designs backgrounds and sets up scenes for each shot; works closely with the props department	Creative
Newspaper editor	In charge of the overall look and content of a newspaper, making sure that it is factually correct and free of errors	Editorial
Editor (television, film)	Requires a sound use of technical skills and a good knowledge of current digital technology available in the chosen field	Editorial
Station manager	Responsible for the operation, administration, scheduling and regulation of a radio station	Managerial
Floor manager	Controls the floor of a set and links the studio to the control room	Managerial
Public relations officer	Works to ensure that the 'public image' of a person or company is represented the way they want to be viewed by the public	Sales and marketing
Film promoter	Makes sure all new releases are well publicised so the public knows about them and when they will be released	Sales and marketing
Publicist	Organises publicity for people or events to raise public awareness	Sales and marketing
Producer	In charge of the start of the production process; coordinates, supervises and controls matters such as raising funds for the proposed production	Financial

Activity: Identification of film crew roles

There are lots of people on a film set, all performing many different job roles; some are technical, some are creative and some are even financial.

Look into a typical crew required to make a film and identify the different job roles that are undertaken.

Once you have identified as many roles as possible, outline and define the skills and knowledge required to do each job. You can do this by conducting your own research, as well as using the table above to help you identify the different skills areas.

Professional working practices

All of the different laws and codes of conduct are put in place to ensure that the consumer receiving the products and services that the industry provides are protected from things such as:

- unfair treatment
- invasion of privacy
- unsuitable content
- defamation.

They also ensure that all members of society are treated fairly and equally without prejudice or misrepresentation.

Working practices are professional practices and conduct within the creative media sector. They will have an impact on how you work and what you produce, as well as ensuring you are protected and treated fairly in your work environment. Examples of laws and codes of conduct that set out working practices are:

- BBC guidelines
- web accessibility guidelines (W3C)
- press codes of conduct
- advertising standards
- libel laws
- Misuse of Computers Act
- Race Discrimination Act.

Key term

Working practices – professional practices and conduct within the creative media sector.

Activity: Professional conduct

Because the creative media sector creates so many different products, it is important to ensure that the people making these products are aware of and understand the restrictions on working practices.

These restrictions are not there to dampen ideas or creative talents, but rather to protect us all from unscrupulous practices. For example, a person working in web development may be able to gain access to personal files and data belonging to others. What law would stop them from accessing and using those data? Why is it important that people aren't allowed to access this information?

If a newspaper decides to write an article about a famous person and chooses to go to their house and take photos of them, what is to stop them from taking pictures through the celebrity's bedroom window? What codes of conduct exist that dictate how the press should behave? Why do you think it is important that a journalist cannot just write what they want about someone?

You have been given some examples of professional codes of conduct and the types of laws that exist. Do research of your own into some of these and answer the questions below.

- Why do they exist?
- Who do they protect?
- Why do they affect your work?

Once you have done your research this is an excellent topic to use in class discussions. You may be surprised at the different views of your class mates!

As you can see, there are a few rules and regulations that you will have to abide by when working in the creative media sector, and this is no different to jobs in other industries. We all have to be aware of legal and ethical issues within our workplaces, however, media producers need to be mindful of how their products will be represented and interpreted by the public.

Case study: Jonathan Ross and Russell Brand

An example of codes of conduct being broken is the scandal of 2008, in which Russell Brand and Jonathan Ross were involved in leaving messages that contained inappropriate content on Andrew Sachs' answering machine. This infamous incident resulted in numerous complaints and an Ofcom investigation. Russell Brand resigned from the BBC, Jonathan Ross was suspended without pay, and the BBC was fined £150,000. They were not the only people to suffer as a result of the scandal: the production staff involved were also disciplined or asked to leave the company.

- What professional codes of conduct did the programme producers infringe?
- Who do you think was responsible for these infringements?
- Could the Ofcom fines have been avoided?
- What steps do you think a company could make to avoid these problems occurring in the future?

Contracts, conditions and pay

All employers, no matter which industry they are in, will provide you with a contract of employment that outlines your work pattern – the days, hours and times you will work – and details the amount you can expect to get paid for the work you do.

As you can imagine, there are many different types of employment contract available and this is due to the fact that a company has to employ people to suit its needs.

In the creative media sector there is a huge emphasis on flexibility, as production processes can be long and drawn out over unsociable hours. For example, 24-hour news channels broadcast live, day and night, to ensure that they provide the latest breaking news. Flexibility can also be important in order to stay ahead of new developments, styles, trends, social issues and so on. As a result, media producers need to ensure that new, up-and-coming talents are taken on in all areas of the business, as and when necessary. It is important to remember that most creative media industries work on a global basis, covering many different time zones that will be in front of or behind UK time. If you want to talk to someone in the USA at the start of the day, you may have to be up at 1 a.m. UK time to do so.

Case study: Working hours limits and the creative media sector

The UK government has set guidelines on employment terms and conditions, including a limit on the number of hours an employee can be contracted to work in a week. The guidelines state that an employee should not have to work more than 48 hours a week on average, unless they choose to do so or work in a sector with its own rules. If a person chooses to opt out of the 48-hour limit, it must be voluntary and in writing.

Working hours and conditions are a hotly debated topic in the creative media sector. The industry has a high proportion of self-employed workers, who are often not covered by the same provisions as employed workers, and it is not uncommon for them to accept lower fees and conditions.

Trade unions work hard to get better conditions for their members. For example, Equity represents artists from across the entire spectrum of arts and entertainment. Its members benefit from minimum terms and conditions across the entertainment industry and guidelines for work in areas where there are no representative bodies.

- Why do you think some creative media employers ask their employees to opt out of the working hours limits?

- Do you think it is realistic for an employee to refuse a request to opt out of the working hours limits from their employer?

- Can you find any examples within the creative media sector where people have been injured as a result of working long hours?

How has the globalisation of the creative media sector altered the ways in which you may be required to work?

Because the needs of a creative media producer can shift and change on a regular basis, more 'flexible' contracts are used than in any other industry. The newspaper industry, for example, uses a lot of freelance photographers as the demand for the all-important celebrity 'snap' is so high that they need people available at all times, all over the world. These contracts are often for a fixed period of time and are not always renewed when they run out. You could be commissioned to write a script for a sitcom, but if the show is cancelled then so is your contract. Some examples of these contracts and pay conditions, as well as a brief description of what they mean, have been provided for you.

- **Full-time, permanent** – as the name suggests, you work on a full-time basis, usually 39 hours a week. A permanent contract means you are a regular member of staff entitled to company benefits including pensions, sick pay, maternity/paternity leave and holiday pay.

- **Part-time, permanent** – this means you work a fraction of a full-time post, but again you will have a set amount of hours per week. You will also be entitled to those benefits outlined above, but on a reduced basis due to working fewer hours.

- **Fixed-term and freelance** – these contracts are similar in that they are both temporary and will only last for a certain period of time. Under a fixed-term contract you may still be entitled to company benefits if outlined in your contract. However, a freelance worker will be responsible for their own arrangements in terms of pension, holiday and sick pay and other allowances. They also have to take care of paying their own tax and National Insurance.

- **Shift work** – this means your hours are set to a certain time of the day, for example, 7 a.m.–3 p.m. or 11 p.m.–7 a.m. Shifts can include late or night work and are often used in places that need to be manned 24 hours a day, such as broadcasting centres.

- **Office hours** – traditionally, these are Monday–Friday, 9 a.m.–5 p.m. and are very common for people working in administration and office-based jobs.

- **Irregular and anti-social hours pay** – this is quite common in the creative media industries, as production work, especially on location, can be irregular and may involve working very early in the morning or late in to the night. These payments are an incentive to people to work these unsociable hours above and beyond their normal contracted duties.

- **Salaried** – a set annual wage that is broken down into monthly payments. A salary will be advertised as, for example, £20,000 per annum, meaning per year, this is then divided by 12 to give you a monthly payment of around £1,666 – don't forget that you will have to pay tax and National Insurance on this!

- **On completion** – this is also quite common in the creative media industries, especially for people commissioned to do work. A contract outlines what you are required to do and by when, and you will be paid the agreed fee when the work is completed.

Remember

Many people start work in a creative media industry on a voluntary basis, so be prepared to work hard for little financial reward to start off with. The important thing to do at this stage is to network with people and make contacts; sometimes it is who you know. Keep your eye on the ultimate goal and be ready to work hard for what you want.

BTEC Assessment activity 3.2

This learning outcome is designed to help you understand the different job roles available in your chosen field and to give you an insight into the types of employment contracts and working conditions you are likely to experience.

Imagine you are looking for work as a games designer. Research the different job roles available and the type of contracts and working conditions you can expect to encounter.

- Outline the job roles and conditions of employment in the computer games industry. **P2**

- Describe with some detail the job roles and conditions of employment in the computer games industry and include some appropriate illustrative examples. **M2**

- Explain and evaluate the job roles and conditions of employment in the computer games industry. Refer to precise and detailed examples to illustrate what you are saying. **D2**

Grading tips

To aim for a **merit** grade, you need to be able to effectively describe job roles relevant to your chosen industry, and provide some details about possible working conditions and contracts of employment you might expect to find in that industry, using examples to make your point.

To aim for a **distinction** grade, you need to go a step further and explain all of these issues whilst providing some sound examples that illustrate your point and that are highly relevant to your chosen industry.

PLTS

Planning and carrying out research into job roles and recruitment will help you to develop your skills as an **independent enquirer**.

Functional skills

Making contact with media companies for research purposes using email will help you to improve your **ICT** skills.

3. Know how to gain employment in a creative media industry

This learning outcome is designed to allow you to develop an understanding of the processes that you need to go through in order to gain employment in a creative media industry. You will look at some of the ways in which you can obtain the skills and qualifications needed in the creative media sector. You will also be encouraged to look into and reflect upon your own skills and development and their relevance to your chosen industry. Finally, you will address recruitment methods and pathways and look at ways of finding work within the industry of your choice.

Skills and qualifications

Gaining a good education and undertaking relevant training are all steps that you can take to help acquire the skills you need to work in the creative media sector.

There are many options available and lots of people start off in full-time or part-time education doing vocational qualifications such as this BTEC Level 2 First, or the BTEC Level 3 National Creative Media Production. This will give you a sound insight into the sector and help you to gain the necessary skills for your chosen specialist field. These qualifications can also lead on to graduate and later post-graduate studies, depending on how far you wish to go down the academic route.

Training on the job is another good way of learning new skills, especially for people gaining voluntary work in their chosen area.

This course can be your first step towards a career in a creative media industry. Relevant work experience can also help your career prospects. What else can you do to increase your chances of getting your dream job?

Self-training is also a possibility and, with the many home-accessible software packages available, more and more people are getting involved in editing home movies, manipulating photo images, mixing sound, writing their own blogs and creating their own web pages; some people even create and distribute their own fanzines. The possibilities are endless and any skills gained this way can only help you gain future employment.

Progression routes for creative media production jobs

The following examples show the progression routes of two people working in creative media industries.

Runner to camera operator

Paul started voluntary work as a runner on television productions. He made himself available for work as and when needed and was soon offered paid employment as a camera assistant. As he built up his skills and contacts he was offered work as a camera operator and now works on many productions for Granada Television, including *Coronation Street*.

Runner/researcher to radio producer

Rachael began voluntary work for a local radio station whilst studying a National Diploma at college. Initially she worked as a runner and researcher – being a smaller station she was required to fill multiple roles. Rachael worked her way up and now works as a producer for the afternoon 'drive time' slot, on which she is responsible for scheduling, programme content and ensuring the smooth running of the programme.

Activity: Training for the future

This activity requires you to assess your current qualifications and get some advice from a local careers advisor.

Research possible progression routes and discuss them with your friends and family to see what they think. Here are some possible progression routes to think about:

- runner – camera assistant – camera operator (television and film)
- BTEC ND Creative Media Production– degree in English – journalist (print)
- researcher – production assistant – producer (television and radio)
- advertising degree – unpaid internship – advertising executive.

Sometimes it is a good idea to get professional advice, so why not make an appointment with the careers advisor to discuss your options?

Finally, have a look at the websites of media companies and make a note of the skills and qualifications they look for in prospective job candidates.

Transferable skills

Transferable skills are those skills that cross over into many different areas of work and life. For example, **personal attributes** – parts of your personality and who you are – may be relevant to a particular job. If you are an ideas person you may find that writing scripts and coming up with new programme concepts will suit you as a career choice. If you are meticulous, organised and able to get things done you may find a production role will suit you best.

There are other personal attributes that will serve you well in life and work, such as the ability to **commit** yourself wholly to what you do, at all times.

Efficiency and **reliability** are also very important, as an employer needs to know they can rely on you to turn up for work when you are needed and that you will do your job well and without constant supervision. Think also about **punctuality**, as this will affect your reliability. You can't turn up late for work on a regular basis with a list of excuses; you need to be there on time, day after day. This may seem obvious and, of course, these are important skills to have in any job, however, in the creative media sector you will always be working to deadlines and reliability is of great importance.

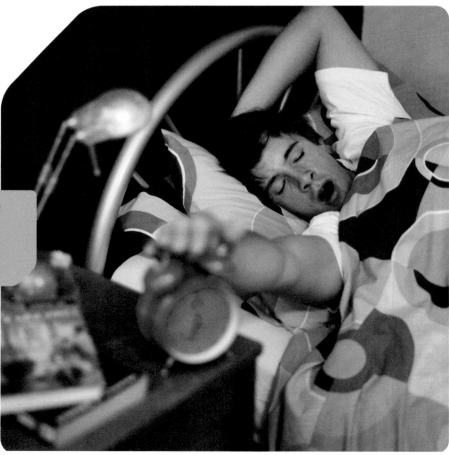

Punctuality is important in almost any career. Are you good at meeting deadlines and being on time or is this something you will need to work on?

Activity: Self–appraisal

Carry out a self appraisal: look at yourself and your skills and analyse their importance and relevance. Your responses to this exercise will give you a good understanding of your strengths and weaknesses and can also form the basis of your CV.

1. First look at your personal attributes and skills. List them in order of how significant you think they are to your chosen industry.

2. Next, look in detail at the sort of job you would like to gain in your chosen industry. Make a list of the most important skills and attributes you will need to do this job.

3. Now match your skills to those relevant to your chosen job. How well matched are you to your chosen career? Are their areas that you need to improve? What can you do to make these improvements and where can you gain these necessary skills?

A self appraisal is all about being honest with yourself and assessing your own personal strengths and weaknesses. Although it can be hard at times to admit to these weaknesses, this is an important part of the training process; after all, skills can always be gained and weaknesses can become strengths if you work at them.

Think about it

The recruitment process in all media industries is competitive. There will be a lot of people going for the same job, so you need to be able to sell yourself to any prospective employer. Think of ways in which you can do this.

Methods of recruitment

There are many places to go to look for jobs. Even the most obvious, the job centre, is never a bad idea as some national companies will put adverts out nationwide. There are also occasions where, for example, television companies will advertise for up-and-coming talent after one of their programmes.

With most people though, the search for a job will usually start on the Internet. This is because local and national companies within the creative media sector, such as the BBC, Channel 4 or even your local radio station, will often have a website and they will use this as a means of advertising job vacancies.

Another good place to look for work is in the local and national press, as they will advertise general jobs available in the local area, as well as specific jobs in industry sectors. *The Guardian* every Monday has a specific section relating to recruitment in the creative media sector. There are also publications called **trade press**, such as *Game Developer* magazine, which are specific to certain sectors of the industry and often run details of current vacancies.

A final method to think about is word of mouth. Talk to people and see if they have heard of any jobs going in the local area or have seen an advert that is not relevant to them but could be of interest to you. Alternatively, it may be that you or somebody you know has personal contacts within your chosen industry and may be willing to recommend you for a position within their company.

Look through a selection of newspapers and make a note of the different jobs available, as well as the skills and qualifications required for each one. Do any of them particularly appeal to you?

EMPLOYMENT

Activity: Job search

Try undertaking some job searches of your own. Look at local and national companies within the creative media sector and search their websites to see if they have any links to recruitment opportunities. Most companies will have something, even if it is just a contact number for their personnel department.

Sometimes it is easier to search in a newspaper, as you can make notes on the page as you go along and circle jobs that are of interest to you.

1. First make a list of the types of jobs you are looking for.

2. It is also beneficial to consider a geographical area you want to work in, namely, how far you are willing to travel for work and how realistic travelling is to your personal circumstances.

3. Make a note of any jobs you find that meet your requirements and outline why.

4. Finally, draft a cover letter to one of the companies you have chosen outlining yourself and your skills and your reasons for applying for the job.

Assessment activity 3.3

For most people, making the right decisions about their qualification and training needs can be quite tricky. For others, it is a simple choice driven by underlying factors such as a desire to work in a certain field.

Think about where you are now – the qualifications you have, and the grades you are likely to obtain in your current course. Use this assessment activity to think about where you want to be in the future. It is always best to make plans that will last over the long term; after all, this is a life choice that you are making.

Write up the results of your research and skills analysis, outlining why you have chosen your particular progression route, how it is relevant to your chosen career and where you plan to look for work.

- Outline how to obtain employment in your chosen industry within the creative media sector. **P3**

- Describe in some detail how to obtain employment in your chosen industry sector and include some appropriate illustrative examples. **M3**

- Explain and evaluate how to obtain employment in your chosen industry sector with reference to precise and detailed illustrative examples. **D3**

Grading tips

To aim for a **merit** grade, you need to provide some sound examples of progression routes in your chosen industry sector, giving examples of skills, education and training, and recruitment pathways.

To aim for a **distinction** grade, you need to be more detailed in your examples and explain progression routes in your chosen industry sector, giving detailed examples of skills, education and training, and recruitment pathways.

PLTS

Analysing and evaluating research information, judging its relevance and value to proposed assignments, will help you to develop your skills as an **independent enquirer**.

Functional skills

Presenting results of research in an appropriate format will help to improve your **ICT** skills.

Paul Franklin

Freelancer in the television industry

I began my television career working as a runner for Granada Satellite and Men and Motors. This was a great training ground, as it allowed me to try out different jobs, including researcher and presenter. I moved on to the camera department and got promoted to mainstream studio-based programmes, including *A Question of Sport* and *You've Been Framed*. I was also a camera operator for local news and a camera assistant for ITV drama.

My first job was unpaid. I answered an advert for runners on a series being filmed in the local area. They were long hours, but the experience was invaluable. I was asked to work for another five days, this time in London, which I accepted. This then led to an offer of paid work at studios in Manchester.

As a result, I was employed by Granada on a full-time basis, which meant getting holiday and sick pay, but it was restrictive in terms of money and choice of projects. After four years, I went freelance, which gave me more freedom, but meant I had to work harder to establish industry contacts. A lot of the time was spent on the phone setting up the next job! However, being freelance can lead to more opportunities and is how most people in the industry work.

The best part of the job is enjoying what you do and being surrounded by others who feel the same way. The worst part is the hours.

Getting a start in this industry is all about networking and patience. You need to meet people and show your face. That means ringing production companies, looking for location production shoots and making general enquiries. From there, it is about keeping enthusiastic, offering help and asking questions constantly. Although you may not get paid at first, people in the industry soon become aware of potential employees. You just need to be patient.

Think about it

1. How many different job roles has Paul undertaken?
2. Can you identify some different contracts of employment?
3. What are the key skills Paul has outlined as being required in his industry?

Just checking

1. Name four different types of media ownership.
2. Outline what is meant by the term 'cross-media ownership'.
3. Can you name any cross-media companies?
4. Why is it important that ownership of the media is spread across a range of media producers?
5. What are transferable skills? How will they help you gain employment in the creative media sector?
6. How important is education and training when looking for work? Which do you think is more important, or do you think that they are equally important?
7. When job hunting, what are the key points to remember?
8. Can you list any of the major websites or publications that are available for recruitment into the creative media sector?
9. Why are legal restrictions on media production important?
10. Can you recall what legal and ethical restrictions exist in the following media industries?
    a. Television
    b. Multimedia
    c. Press
11. What are the potential consequences of ignoring the codes of practice?
12. Write down five reasons why it is important for you to fully understand and comply with the codes of practice of your chosen industry sector.

Assignment tips

- When looking at media ownership, carry out a detailed research into the ownership and any subsidiaries of an individual company to give you a better understanding of their interests within the creative media sector.
- Keep references of searches that you have made in newspapers and on websites, especially web addresses, so that you know where you have been looking and can refer back to anything of interest for more information.
- Update your CV on a regular basis to ensure that all relevant skills and training have been included. Be sure to write a targeted CV, which focuses on the relevant skills and training for the type of jobs you are interested in.
- Target your job searches around your skills; aim for jobs that are relevant to what you know you can do. The best way to do this is to look at the personal specification, which details what the company are looking for, and try to match yourself to that.
- Take on voluntary work when and wherever possible, especially at this time when you are most able to afford working for free, as this will provide you with invaluable training and experience.
- Keep focused on your education and training, as this will help you to gain employment in the future. Keep your education and training relevant to your areas of interest and target them to suit your needs.

4 Media audiences and products

Media products do not exist in isolation. The films and television programmes that we watch, the radio stations and podcasts that we listen to, the newspapers and magazines that we read and the websites and computer games that we interact with are all trying to get our attention in today's busy media marketplace.

It is a highly competitive world and media companies need to have a very detailed and thorough understanding of their audience if they are to stand a chance of success. Constructing their products in such a way that they are able to target the right product at the right audience in the right way is important for all media producers.

This unit provides you with the opportunity to learn how a media industry identifies and finds out about the audience for its products. You will also learn about the factors influencing the ways in which these media products are constructed for their specific target audience. You will then be able to find out how audiences respond to these media products.

Learning outcomes

After completing this unit you should:

1. know how a media industry identifies audiences for its products
2. understand how media products are constructed for specific audiences
3. understand how audiences can respond to media products.

Assessment and grading criteria

This table shows you what you must do in order to achieve a **pass**, **merit** or **distinction** grade, and where you can find activities in this book to help you.

To achieve a **pass** grade the evidence must show that you are able to:	To achieve a **merit** grade the evidence must show that, in addition to the pass criteria, you are able to:	To achieve a **distinction** grade the evidence must show that, in addition to the pass and merit criteria, you are able to:
P1 outline ways in which a media industry identifies audiences for its products **See Assessment activity 4.1, page 87**	**M1** describe ways in which a media industry identifies audiences for its products with some detail and with reference to appropriate illustrative examples **See Assessment activity 4.1, page 87**	**D1** explain ways in which a media industry identifies audiences for its products with reference to precise and detailed illustrative examples **See Assessment activity 4.1, page 87**
P2 outline ways in which a media product is constructed for a specific audience **See Assessment activity 4.2, page 97**	**M2** describe ways in which a media product is constructed for a specific audience with some detail and with reference to appropriate illustrative examples **See Assessment activity 4.2, page 97**	**D2** explain ways in which a media product is constructed for a specific audience with reference to precise and detailed illustrative examples **See Assessment activity 4.2, page 97**
P3 outline ways in which a media product might be understood by an audience **See Assessment activity 4.3, page 102**	**M3** describe ways in which a media product might be understood by an audience with some detail and with reference to appropriate illustrative examples **See Assessment activity 4.3, page 102**	**D3** explain ways in which a media product might be understood by audiences with reference to precise and detailed illustrative examples **See Assessment activity 4.3, page 102**

How you will be assessed

This unit will be assessed using a number of internal assignments that will be designed and marked by the tutors at your centre. These may be subject to sampling by your centre's External Verifier as part of Edexcel's ongoing quality assurance procedures.

The assignments are designed to allow you to show your understanding of the unit outcomes. These relate to what you should be able to do after completing this unit. Most of the assignments that you will complete for this unit will relate to work that you are doing in some of your other units, particularly the work that you will be undertaking in Unit 1 Research for creative media production, and in the optional practical production units.

Your assessments could be in the form of:

- presentations
- case studies
- practical tasks
- written assignments.

Natasha, Video production

The main thing this unit taught me was how important the audience are to media production companies. They need to know as much information about their target audience as possible so that they can make sure the products they create are the ones the target audience want.

Media production companies also need this information so that they can tell other people about their audience, particularly advertisers, as they need them to advertise the correct products in their films, programmes, magazines and websites for the particular target audience.

This had a big impact on my own practical production work because it made me realise that I had to think very carefully about who I was making my media products for. It also reminded me that I needed to undertake my own research into my target audience so that they would be happy with the products I was making for them.

I enjoyed finding out how media products are constructed and it made me think more carefully about planning and pre-production. Before doing the unit, I was impatient and just wanted to pick up a camera and make a recording. Now I understand that to make a successful recording I need to know who I am making it for and think carefully about all the different parts that go into a successful product.

- What parts of this unit do you think you will enjoy the most?
- What support might you need to complete this unit?
- What can you do to prepare yourself for the unit assessments?

1. Know how a media industry identifies audiences for its products

Media consumers

We are all **consumers** of media products. But what do you know about the people around you?

Working in pairs, ask your partner about themselves, their lifestyle and their media consumption. Divide your questions up so that you find out what products they consume within the different creative media industry sectors. For example, for television you may want to find out:

- how much television they watch a week
- whether they have cable, satellite or Freeview
- whether they have a television set in their bedroom
- what their favourite television programmes are.

Use their answers to build up a profile of the person as a media consumer.

Discuss your findings with your partner and then present the profile to the rest of the class.

Are you surprised at what you find out about the people around you or do they all fit into a familiar profile?

Key term

Profile – a set of information that summarises what a person is like.

The products that the creative media industries create are all designed for a specific audience. All commercial media products have to contend in a very competitive media marketplace. Targeting the right product at the right audience in the right way is an important skill that all media producers must develop if their particular product is going to survive.

How many people in your class have a television in their bedroom? Are you surprised by this figure?

Classification of audiences

Media producers need to know as much information about their audience – the **media consumers** – as possible. The UK has over 60 million people, all of whom are potential audience members for a particular media product.

Did you know?

Black and white television images of the moon landing were watched by an estimated 600 million people worldwide in July 1969. At the time, this represented almost a fifth of the world's population.

On 22 August 2008, over 680 million people in mainland China tuned into one of the country's four major sports television channels showing full colour coverage of the Beijing Olympics. This represented 56 per cent of China's television audience.

What do these two pieces of information tell you about the growth in television broadcasting over the last 40 years?

Some target audiences are quite broad. For example, television listings magazines are potentially targeting everybody who watches television, and coverage of a large sporting event such as the Olympic Games will be targeting a **mass market**. Some products are targeted at a much narrower, specialised target audience and this is often referred to as a **niche market**.

Dividing the potential audience into different categories makes it easier for a media producer to identify and target people with similar needs and expectations.

In Unit 1 you would have found out that media researchers are interested in dividing the audience into four key categories:

- age
- gender
- culture
- social class.

In this unit, we are also interested in these four categories and will add some more:

- lifestyle
- location
- sexual orientation.

Key term

Media consumer – somebody who watches, listens to, reads or interacts with a media product.

Key terms

Mass market – a large target audience that is not very well defined or segmented.

Niche market – a small, well-defined, specialised target audience.

Key terms

Psychographics – the study of people based on their attitudes, opinions and lifestyle.

Geodemographics – the study of people based on where they live.

Demographics – the study of people according to factors like age, gender and ethnicity.

Lifestyle

Psychographics are used to classify people according to their attitudes, opinions and lifestyle. Information about a person's attitudes, opinions and lifestyle is important to advertisers and media producers as it will give them important clues as to what interests the person has, how much disposable income they are likely to have and what type of media products they are likely to be attracted to.

For example, people who lead an active lifestyle are likely to be attracted to media products that reflect a similar lifestyle; advertisers of travel-related products, health foods and sports equipment may be interested in advertising to these people via such products.

Location

Location is also important to media producers and advertisers. **Geodemographics** are used to classify people according to where they live, sometimes organised by their postcode. Companies who are producing media products for a local or regional audience need to know how many people live in the area they are targeting and what percentage live in the countryside, as well as the towns and cities in the area.

Demographics are used to describe a group of people according to factors such as age, gender, ethnicity, social class and sexual orientation. Knowing the profile of the local and regional population can help a local newspaper or regional radio station to provide the right content to appeal to their target audience.

A magazine is targeted at a specific niche audience. Have a look at a selection of lifestyle magazines and see whether you can identify any link between the adverts within them and the magazine's target audience.

Case study: Andover Sound

Andover Sound is an independent radio station broadcasting from studios in Andover to listeners in North West Hampshire.

Like all commercial radio stations, Andover Sound gets most of its income from selling advertising space in and around its radio shows. It is a competitive market and the station has to compete with other local radio programmes, the local press, commercial television and the Internet for advertising revenue.

To compete successfully, it has to understand who its listeners are and what they want, and promote itself to local businesses who are potential advertisers.

One key aspect of Andover Sound's marketing to local businesses is that their radio station reaches out to the right local audience. They have researched their local listeners and stress the point that commercial radio listeners tend to be younger than local newspaper readers, have families and spend more on shopping.

- Why is geodemographics so important for Andover Sound?
- Do some research into one of your local commercial radio stations. What does it say about its audience?
- What other media products is the station competing with for advertising revenue?

Sexual orientation

In the past, many representations of lesbian, bisexual and homosexual people in the media were very negative and often limited to common stereotypes. Today the situation is much more positive and many media products have characters that represent a more positive and realistic image of people's sexual orientation.

This is partly to do with changes in social attitudes towards sexual orientation, changes in the laws on discrimination and the realisation by media companies that analysing their audience according to sexual orientation is another way in which they can accurately target the right product at the right audience.

Profile

One of the reasons that media producers are interested in dividing the audience up in these ways is so that they can get a better idea of the profile of their typical target audience.

This profile can then be used to help media producers who are operating within a commercial market to sell advertising space in and around their media products.

Think about it

Even non-commercial media producers such as the BBC are interested in the profile of their target audience. Why might this be?

All media producers are interested in knowing as much about their target audience as possible because this information can help them to design and create the sorts of programmes, films, websites, computer games, magazines and newspapers that they think the audience wants.

PLTS

Collaborating with other members of your class when analysing the adverts will help you to develop your skills as a **team worker**.

Functional skills

Presenting your findings to the rest of the class will help you to develop your **English** skills in speaking and listening.

Activity: Advertising in newspapers

1. Working in small groups, choose three different national newspapers.

2. Look through each paper and write a list of the types of product or service that are advertised within each one.

3. Cut out some examples of the adverts from each paper and use these to produce a poster for each newspaper that summarises the advertising within it.

4. Visit the National Readership Survey (NRS) website and find out the social profile for each paper. To obtain a link to the NRS website, please see the Hotlinks section on page ii.

5. Describe the relationship between the social profile and the advertising that you have discovered.

6. Present your findings to the rest of the class.

What sort of audience is an advertisement of this type trying to attract? What type of magazine do you think it might appear in?

IMPULSION
THE NEW FRAGRANCE FOR WOMEN

Audience research

Media organisations undertake audience research to find out information about their target audience using a selection of the main research methods and techniques that you found out about in Unit 1.

Media organisations use primary research techniques such as focus groups, questionnaires and face-to-face interviews. They also use secondary research by obtaining ratings and circulation figures from specialised media research organisations that produce their own data to sell on to advertisers and production companies.

One specialist form of primary research that these organisations often use is the audience measurement panel. This is a group of people who have been hand-picked to represent the audience as a whole. The products that they watch, listen to or interact with are monitored and recorded and the resulting data is used to produce estimates of what the rest of the UK population are watching, listening to and interacting with.

Case study: The Broadcasters' Audience Research Board

The Broadcasters' Audience Research Board (BARB) is the organisation responsible for providing the official measurement of television audiences in the UK. The figures produced are based on estimates of the number of people watching television.

Viewing estimates are obtained from an audience reporting panel of 5,200 homes that represent the viewing behaviour of the 26 million homes that have a television in the UK. The panel is selected to be representative of each ITV and BBC region. On average, each panel member represents about 5,000 members of the UK's population.

When a household joins the panel, all of the television sets within it are monitored by a meter that electronically records what is being watched. The meter is a small box, which sits next to each television set and automatically collects information about the channel that the television set is receiving.

Throughout the day, the meter system stores all viewing undertaken by the entire household. Every night, these data are downloaded from every panel home and processed before being released to the industry at 9.30 the following morning. These minute-by-minute reports are known as 'overnights' and include any recorded material played back on the

same day as the original transmission. Overnight data provide the first report of how the previous day's programming and advertising have performed.

Any time-shifted recording and playback that takes place within 7 days of the original broadcast is added to the live data to produce the final, minute-by-minute audience figures. These viewing data are referred to as 'consolidated' data and serve as the official 'BARB Gold Standard' that is used by the industry for reporting and trading.

Channels reported by BARB provide timings of the programmes and commercials they broadcast. These records are then matched to the minute-by-minute viewing data to produce the BARB official audience viewing estimates for each individual programme and commercial.

- Visit the BARB website and have a look at the latest data it has produced. To obtain a link to the BARB website, please see the Hotlinks section on page ii.

- What was the average amount of time that a person watched television last week?

- Which channel was the most popular?

Commercial television companies are very interested in the data that BARB produces, and so are potential advertisers who want to advertise their products and services within their programmes. As more and more channels become available, the audience becomes more fragmented between them, so advertisers have to work even harder to make sure they are reaching the right people with their adverts.

Activity: Television advertising

1. Watch a number of commercial television programmes tonight.
2. Write down the name and type of each programme you watch.
3. Make a note of the products and services that are advertised during the commercial breaks for each programme.
4. Produce a chart of your findings and present your results to the rest of the class.
5. Can you see a clear link between the adverts and the programme within which they appear?

When you're watching television, look out for programmes that are sponsored by a company. Is there a link between the type of programme and the company that has sponsored it?

Assessment activity 4.1 P1 M1 D1

You work for a research company that specialises in providing audience data for the creative media sector. You have been asked to give a short presentation to shareholders at the annual general meeting in which you outline the ways in which one of the media industries identifies audiences for its products.

- Choose one media industry and, in your own words, describe the main ways in which the industry identifies audiences for its media products. **P1**
- Include some detailed examples of how your chosen industry identifies audiences for its media products. **M1**
- Explain and try to evaluate the ways in which your chosen industry identifies audiences for its media products. Include precise and detailed examples to support what you are saying. **D1**

Grading tips

To aim for a **merit** grade, your description needs to be detailed, including at least two specific examples that help to support what you are saying about the ways in which your chosen industry identifies audiences for its media products.

To aim for a **distinction** grade, you need to go beyond description and begin to explain in some depth the methods used. You should support what you are saying with precise and detailed examples.

 PLTS

Investigating the ways in which your chosen media industry identifies audiences for its products will help you to develop your skills as an **independent enquirer**.

 Functional skills

Outlining the ways in which your chosen media industry identifies audiences for its products will help you to develop your **English** skills in writing.

2. Understand how media products are constructed for specific audiences

Knowing about your audience is an important first step to a successful media production. However, media producers need to put this information to good use when they begin to plan and develop the media products they are going to create for this audience.

Elements of construction

When planning the construction of any media product there are three key elements that you need to consider:

- selection
- composition
- combination.

 Remember

You will be creating your own media productions in some of your other units. You too will need to use your knowledge and understanding of your target audience to help you plan and develop your own successful products.

Selection

The process of researching and gathering material for a media product will generate a lot of information and material – far too much to fit into the final product. One of the skills that you need to develop is the ability to select the right material for your final product and reject the rest.

One of the best ways in which you can see this selection process in action is to visit the newsroom of your local newspaper or your local television news broadcaster. The newsroom will receive hundreds of stories and potential leads from a variety of different sources. The editor for the paper or news broadcast will have to decide quickly which stories he or she wants the journalists to follow up and which ones will be put to one side.

Case study: BBC News Centre

Selecting which stories will make the news and which will not is particularly important for a national news organisation like the BBC that is required to provide an accurate and high-quality public service to its viewers and listeners.

BBC News is the largest broadcast news operation in the world, with more than 2,000 journalists gathering information from a range of different sources.

All of this material needs to be carefully sorted and checked for accuracy and suitability before being rewritten and reworked into the range of different news-related programmes that the BBC produces. In 2008, the BBC produced more than 45,000 hours of news-related programming for television and radio.

BBC News is also a global news provider, reaching more than 260 million viewers through the international television news channel BBC World and more than 150 million listeners via BBC World Service.

At the heart of the operation is the BBC News Centre in West London. The newsroom works round the clock, every day of the year, producing news stories for all of its programmes. It is very varied work and the journalists can be writing for lots of different channels and stations at the same time, producing short headlines for BBC Radio 2, and then compiling half-hour bulletins for BBC Radio 4.

Where does the news come from? Every newsroom journalist uses a computer system called Essential News Production System (ENPS). This connects BBC staff all over the country and in offices around the world. It carries the latest information from British and international news agencies, such as the Press Association and Reuters, so all editorial staff have up-to-the-minute news at their desks.

In addition, BBC reporters and correspondents at home and abroad can be called on for expert coverage across a range of different subject areas.

- What skills does a BBC journalist need?
- Why is it important that they check where the information for news stories has come from?
- Why do they need to produce different news stories for different programmes?

Composition and combination

When creating your media product, the material that you have selected needs to be structured and composed into the correct form and combined with other elements to produce the finished product.

A television news production team needs to structure its stories and features into a broadcast that exactly fits the slot that the channel has provided. Too long and it will crash into the adverts or next programme. Too short and there will be a few seconds of embarrassed silence, or even a blank screen, until the next programme starts.

News broadcasts have a familiar structure to them. After the title sequence, the presenters will introduce the main headlines and then report on each of the stories in turn, starting with what is considered to be the most important or most serious one. They often finish with a humorous story before the weather and then a final summary of the main headlines.

This structure is understood and expected by the audience, who would be surprised and perhaps a little confused if a really important news story was left to the end of the broadcast and they started off with a more trivial one.

Many news programmes now include live location broadcasts from the scene of a news story. Why might they have introduced this new technique into the structure?

Live from Westminster   12.30

Activity: Local television

A good way of looking at how the elements of construction can make a difference to the final product is to look in detail at a specific media programme. In this activity, you will be looking at a local news programme in detail and trying to see the ways in which it has been constructed.

1. Watch (and record if you can) tonight's local early evening television news broadcast.
2. Write a brief description of each news story that features in the show.
3. Count up the number of news stories and features. Are you surprised by the number that you have? Do you think that this is all that happened in your area today? Why do you think these particular stories have been chosen by the news team over any others?
4. Look at the way the programme has been composed. Does it follow the familiar structure described above or have the producers introduced something new to try to be a bit different from the rest?
5. Have a look at the local newspaper the day after the television news broadcast. Are there any news stories that are in both the newspaper and the television programme? Are there any that are only in one of them? Why might this be?

Similar elements are often used to construct a television news story. They will often start with the news presenter sitting in the studio, looking directly at the camera, introducing the story live to the audience. The director will then cut to a pre-recorded sequence to illustrate the story and will often include an interview with somebody connected to the story, along with some moving footage of the event or location.

Modes of address

The **mode of address** refers to the way in which a media product communicates to its audience. The type of language that is used is one important factor.

- Is the language formal or informal?
- Does it use Standard English or colloquial words?
- If it is spoken language, is it shouted or whispered?
- Is the tone harsh or soft?
- Is the accent a regional one or does it sound quite neutral?

Key term

Mode of address – the way in which a media product communicates to its audience.

Look at the two headlines below, together with the opening sentences. Both report on the same news story, but the second one is much more informal than the first.

England Through To World Cup Finals

A dynamic England qualified in style for next year's World Cup finals in South Africa as they defeated Croatia at Wembley.

WE'RE GOING TO SOUTH AFRICA!

MIGHTY England whitewashed Croatia in last night's 5–1 goalathon at Wembley to book their place in next summer's World Cup finals. The Three Lions' ferocious form suggests they'll be prowling for victory in South Africa.

> What type of newspaper do you think each headline would appear in?

Mode of address is not just about language though. Media products also communicate through a range of other ways. The visual imagery in a moving-image programme, website or printed product can be used by a media producer to communicate important information to the audience, and this is often linked to the **genre** (or type of product) that the producer is working with.

A media product can also communicate through the way in which the information put across to the audience is structured. This is often referred to as **narrative structure** and different narrative structures are used to appeal to different audiences.

For example, a soap opera such as *Hollyoaks* or *EastEnders* needs to attract a mass audience who have lots of different interests. Each episode of the soap will usually have lots of different storylines that are designed to appeal to different sections of the audience. If a storyline about a character losing their job doesn't appeal to the younger age group then there is likely to be another storyline, perhaps about a romantic relationship, in the same episode that will. This use of lots of different storylines in a single episode to appeal to a mass audience is called a **multi-strand narrative**.

In soaps, the storylines also carry on into the next episode and this is called an **open narrative**. This encourages the audience to watch the next episode, as they want to find out what happens.

This is different from watching a film where the story is usually closed at the end of the film and it is clear what has happened. This is called a **closed narrative** and is used to clearly indicate the end of the film with no loose ends left. This type of narrative is also used in live sports broadcasting, for example, when the programme ends after the final whistle has blown, and not before!

Key term

Genre – French word meaning 'type'.

Activity: Computer games

Compare the packaging for two computer games. Discuss them with a partner and outline the ways the producer of the games has used visual imagery to communicate a certain message to the audience.

Think about it

Can you think of any films that leave the story open at the end? Why might the producers of the film have used this type of narrative structure? How do you think this makes the audience feel?

Key term

Codes and conventions – a set of elements and characteristics that help to define a particular type of media product.

Genre

The word 'genre' is a French word meaning 'type'. It is used within the creative industries to refer to a distinct type of product. For example, in the television industry there are many different types, or genres, of programmes produced. Each genre has its own set of **codes and conventions**, which help to define it and distinguish it from other genres.

Activity: Television genres

The table below lists some familiar television genres. For two of these genres, the name of a current television programme within that genre has been added, together with a brief summary of the main codes and conventions that help to define it.

1. Make a copy of the table and fill in the missing boxes for the other three genres.

2. Discuss television genres with the rest of the class and then add in at least another five genres to the table, together with the name of a current television programme within each of the genres listed and a brief summary of the main codes and conventions.

Genre	Example	Codes and conventions	Way they appeal to target audience
Soap opera	*Hollyoaks*	A number of realistic storylines follow on to the next episode	Audience can relate to at least some of the storylines
		Each episode lasts about half an hour	Short enough to watch each day
		A weekly omnibus edition shows a week's worth of episodes	Omnibus edition allows audience to catch up with any missed episodes
		No special effects	Doesn't distract from sense of realism
News programme	*News at Ten*	Presenters in a studio	Makes programme look authoritative
		Starts with headlines of main stories – most serious stories first, sport and a humorous story at the end; includes the weather	Structure gives audience a flavour of main stories and helps them to understand which are the most serious; humorous stories and weather encourage audience to stay watching to the end
		Pre-recorded and live reports from locations to illustrate most of the stories; some interviews with people connected to stories	Gives audience more information and also different viewpoints of the story; brings them closer to the action
Situation comedy			
Comedy sketch show			
Science fiction			

Generic codes and conventions are useful to media producers, as they act as a sort of guide or template when they are constructing a particular product. They are also useful for the audience, because they help the audience to understand what the product is trying to communicate and how they should react to it.

Sometimes a media producer will break a generic code or convention to make their product stand out. For example, a convention of soap operas is that they have lots of different storylines running in each individual episode. However, occasionally a programme like *EastEnders* will break this convention by having a single storyline for one episode. Have there been any recent examples of this in any of the soaps that you have seen?

Think about it

What information do you think should be kept private?

Case study: *EastEnders*

One example of a soap breaking some of the established generic codes and conventions was an episode of *EastEnders* shown in 2009.

In February 2009, the BBC screened an episode of *EastEnders* that featured an all-black cast for the first time in its 24-year history. The episode featured the character Patrick Trueman sharing his experiences of being a young black man living in 1950s Britain.

The BBC received almost 250 complaints from viewers, with more than 50 of these received before the episode was shown and the rest after the broadcast. The episode attracted an audience of 8.4 million viewers. A BBC spokesperson at the time said that most of the complaints were from people who felt it was 'inappropriate' for the channel to have shown an episode featuring an all-black cast. Some of the complainants felt it was unnecessary to raise the issue of the Notting Hill race riots in the episode.

In response, the BBC issued a statement saying that it is not unusual for *EastEnders* to devote a whole episode to a single storyline or set of characters. It stated that this episode presented an opportunity to explore the background of one of the soap's most popular characters.

The BBC pointed out that there have been many 'all-white' episodes in the show's history and it sees no reason why an 'all-black' episode should not be included.

- **Which generic conventions did this episode of *EastEnders* break?**
- **Why do you think the producers of the programme decided to do this?**
- **Why do you think some people complained about the episode?**

Constraints

Media producers can't always produce exactly what they want and there are often strict rules and guidelines in place that limit and control what they can produce.

There are certain legal restrictions that apply to all media products. **Copyright restrictions** mean that you cannot copy part of somebody else's work and use it in your own product without asking for permission first. For instance, you may think a song by your favourite band or artist will sound good in the television programme that you are producing, but you will need to get their permission (and probably pay them some money) before you can include it on the soundtrack.

There are also strict laws around **defamation**, **race discrimination** and **data protection** that can limit what information a media product can

Activity: Copyright

The copyright symbol © indicates that a product is protected by copyright laws. Carry out some research to find out how these laws will influence what you can use in your final media product.

Did you know?

In June 2009, the House of Commons was forced, under the Freedom of Information Act, to publish details of MPs' expenses on a website. This followed stories in the *Daily Telegraph* and other parts of the media about some of the expenses claims that were seen to be excessive and others that were thought to be fraudulent.

The revelations led to some MPs resigning and to changes in the way in which the expenses system was run and organised.

contain. However, the law on the freedom of information can often help a newspaper, website, or radio or television documentary team that is trying to report on something that may be a bit controversial.

There are also laws about what you can and can't say about individuals and groups in a particular media product. The **libel law** prevents media producers publishing or broadcasting anything about somebody that is untrue or may damage his or her reputation. Many people have used this law to claim damages against companies that have published damaging or untrue material about them. All large media organisations will take advice from lawyers before publishing or broadcasting anything they think may fall foul of the libel law.

Case study: Keira Knightley

There have been many examples of celebrities and other famous people challenging the media for what it has said or written about them. If they think they have a case then they can take the company that produced the media product to court and try to prove that they have broken a law or gone against an established code of conduct.

Taking a media company to court can be very expensive, as both sides in the argument are likely to employ a legal team to try to argue their case for them.

In 2007, Keira Knightley successfully sued the *Daily Mail* newspaper over remarks it made about her having an alleged eating disorder. She received £3,000 in damages after the *Daily Mail* had published a photograph of the actress on a beach with an accompanying article commenting on her slender figure. Knightley began legal action against the newspaper in January 2007, claiming the article was libellous because it implied she had been dishonest about suffering from anorexia.

The actress has frequently been forced to deny she has an eating disorder, and said that the accusations had left her 'completely devastated'. Keira Knightley also challenged the positioning of the story – published beside an article about a girl who died from anorexia – because it suggested that she was responsible for the teen's death by setting a bad example. Following the ruling at London's High Court in May 2007, the actress said she would donate the money to charity.

- Why do you think Keira Knightley was unhappy with what the newspaper had written about her?
- Why did it break the libel law?
- Why does it tend to be rich and famous people who take media companies to court?

There are codes of practice that relate to specific media industry sectors. You will need to undertake some careful research to find out what the constraints are for the media industry sectors that you want to create products for.

When someone famous takes a publication to court, what is the effect of the consequent publicity on the celebrity and on the publication?

The table below indicates some of the main regulatory bodies that limit and control what an industry sector can and can't produce. To obtain links to their websites and find out more information about what each regulatory body does, please see the Hotlinks section on page ii.

Table 4.1: Industry sectors and the bodies that regulate them. What are some of the constraints that each body imposes?

Industry sector	Regulatory body
Television and radio	Office of Communications (Ofcom)
Film	British Board of Film Classification (bbfc)
Computer games	Pan-European Game Information (PEGI)
Newspapers and magazines	Press Complaints Commission (PCC)
Advertising	Advertising Standards Authority (ASA)
Internet	World Wide Web Consortium (W3C)

The W3C is working to make the Web accessible to all users regardless of differences in culture, education, ability, resources and physical limitations. How is it trying to achieve this?

Case study: The Press Complaints Commission

The PCC is an independent self-regulatory body that deals with complaints about the content of newspapers and magazines and their websites. The PCC's own website includes a comprehensive database of information on complaints it has investigated since 1996. Here is an example of one of these cases.

Case: UK College of Arts & Technology's complaint against the *Daily Mail*

Complaint:

The Director of the UK College of Arts & Technology, Manchester, complained that an article in the *Daily Mail* newspaper about the rise of fraudulent colleges in the UK had made misleading reference to the institution. The Director made it clear that the college was fully accredited, ran legitimate courses and operated a strict enrolments and attendance monitoring procedure in conjunction with the Home Office. He stated that the college should therefore not have been mentioned in the article.

How the complaint was resolved:

The newspaper removed the article from its website and noted the matter on its internal records. It also published a letter from the complainant, which stated the credentials of the college and made it clear that it should not have been included in the article.

- The college was complaining that the *Daily Mail* had breached the terms of the Editors' Code of Practice because it had printed misleading things about it. How was the PCC able to resolve the issue?

- Why might this be seen by both the newspaper and the college as a better solution than going through the courts?

- Do you know of any other examples of investigations by the PCC? Visit its website to find out more (please see the Hotlinks section on page ii).

How can media production companies avoid ending up in court accused of infringement of copyright, libel or defamation laws? What precautions will you need to take when working on your own media product?

Assessment activity 4.2

You are working for a media production company and one of your rival companies has just launched a new product on to the market. Your boss wants the production department to respond to this challenge by launching a new product of your own. In preparation for this, he has asked you to investigate the existing product to find out how it has been constructed.

- Choose one existing media product that has a clearly defined target audience. Investigate the product and, in your own words, describe the main ways in which the product is constructed for its target audience. **P2**

- Include some detailed examples to support your comments about how the product is constructed for its target audience. **M2**

- Explain and try to evaluate how the product is constructed for its target audience. Include precise and detailed examples to support what you are saying. **D2**

Grading tips

To aim for a **merit** grade, your investigation into the existing product needs to be quite thorough and include some specific references to the construction processes used. You also need to identify why these particular processes were used for the target audience.

To aim for a **distinction** grade, your investigation into the existing product needs to be very thorough and you need to go beyond description to explain in detail and depth which processes have been used to construct the product for its target audience. The examples you use should be precise and detailed.

PLTS

Planning and carrying out your investigation into an existing media product will help you to develop your skills as an **independent enquirer**.

Functional skills

Undertaking research via the Internet into the constraints that impact on your chosen media product will help you to develop your **ICT** skills in selecting and using a variety of sources of information.

3. Understand how audiences can respond to media products

Getting the right product in front of the right audience is only half of the battle. For a media product to be successful, the audience has to respond in a positive way to the product by understanding and making sense of it.

Reasons for preference

There are many reasons why somebody will choose a particular media product, or **text**, to **read**. Media texts are often heavily promoted and marketed at a particular group of people, so it is perhaps not surprising that these people will then choose to buy, rent or access this particular text along with thousands, perhaps even millions, of people of the same age, gender, ethnic background and sexual orientation.

Activity: Reasons for choice

Do a quick survey of your class to find out what the top five films, television programmes, computer games and websites are for the girls in the class and then for the boys. Is there any difference in the two lists? Can this difference be explained by choices made according to gender?

Also find out who their favourite DJ is, which website they visit the most and which band or artist they prefer. Again, see if there are any differences that can be explained by gender.

Extension activity

Extend this survey out to the wider community so you can try to include people of a different age, ethnic background and sexual orientation.

It is probably best to devise a short questionnaire for this extended task. Think carefully about what questions you will need to ask at the start of the questionnaire to help you collate the information at the end and check what the different categories of people said.

You will also need to think carefully about how you are going to target a representative sample of each category of person. Discuss this with your tutor and the rest of the class, and put together a plan that will allow you to get the best results.

Carry out the survey, and then collate and analyse your findings.

Language codes

When looking in more depth at the ways in which audiences interact with and respond to media products, the products themselves are often referred to as texts. Magazines, films, television programmes, computer games and websites can all be referred to as texts that are made up of different elements or **codes**. There are **verbal codes** (language), which are spoken; **visual codes**, which are seen by the audience; and **aural codes** (such as music), which are heard by the audience. The act of understanding these codes and getting some meaning from them is often called **reading a text** (even if it involves watching, playing or listening).

Generic codes

When codes link together to help define a particular type of media product, they are called generic codes. You have already seen how generic codes are useful to media producers when they are constructing a particular media text. They are also useful for the audience when they read and try to understand what the text is communicating to them and what meaning they are generating from it.

Some texts will generate happiness, laughter and a feeling of well being. Others might make you feel scared, angry or confused. Identifying and understanding the generic codes in a particular text can make the reading of them easier and more pleasurable for the audience.

For example, if you know that you are watching a situation comedy, you will expect it to contain humorous scenes and some jokes, so you will be ready to laugh. If you are watching a horror film, you will expect to see scenes, characters and action that will shock you and you will expect to feel scared.

Key terms

Code – a set of elements and characteristics that generate meaning for the audience.

Reading a text – a term used within the creative media sector to mean consuming and making sense of a media product.

Horror films often use music to imply danger and make the audience frightened. What other techniques do media production companies use to influence our reactions to their products?

Did you know?

One of the most famous examples of an audience misreading a text was in 1938 when a radio drama production of H.G. Wells' novel *The War of the Worlds* was broadcast.

Although a work of fiction, the story was presented as a series of news bulletins and many listeners thought it was a genuine news broadcast of an invasion by aliens from Mars.

The programme's news bulletin format was criticised by some newspapers at the time, which thought that the audience had been deliberately misled. The resulting publicity was good for the producer of the show, Orson Welles, who went on to become a famous film director.

Orson Welles' 1938 broadcast caused panic among many listeners. If a similar programme were broadcast today, do you think listeners would react in the same way? Why do you think this might be?

There are lots of different codes within a media text that will give the audience clues about what genre it is; these will tell the audience what sort of things they should expect to see and how they should respond.

The table below lists the main types of generic codes and gives an example of what form they may take in a soap opera.

Table 4.2: The generic codes that define the soap opera genre. Think about your favourite soap, does it fulfil all of these codes?

Generic code	How it is used in soap opera
Language	Naturalistic language; accents and dialects linked to the location of the soap
Narrative structure	Multi-strand narrative Open narrative
Characters	Range of everyday characters
Style	Naturalistic style; no special effects
Camera work	Naturalistic camera work
Soundtrack	Naturalistic, everyday sounds
Music	Theme music at start and end but no incidental music on the soundtrack
Mise-en-scène – all of the elements that are put in front of the camera to be filmed, including sets, props, costumes and lighting	Sets, props, costumes and lighting made to look like everyday life
Iconography – how the visual images within a media text can generate meaning	Naturalistic
Graphics	Use of graphics at start and end

Key terms

Mise-en-scène – the elements put in front of the camera to be filmed.

Iconography – how visual images within a media text can generate meaning.

Activity: Generic codes

Reproduce the table above but this time choose a different genre and try to identify how the different generic codes are used within your chosen genre.

Remember, some programmes will deliberately break a generic rule by doing something different. One generic code traditionally used in television news broadcasts was that the newscaster sat behind a desk in the studio. When the new terrestrial channel five started broadcasting, it wanted to appeal to a younger audience and decided to have a young female presenter sitting on a desk reading the news.

 Assessment activity 4.3 (P3) (M3) (D3)

Write an article for a magazine in which you review a specific media product and describe how it may be understood by its audience.

- Choose an existing media product that you can investigate. Use the information that you find to write an article for a magazine in which you review the product and outline ways in which it may be understood by its target audience. (P3)

- Include some detailed examples to support your comments about ways in which the media product may be understood by its target audience. (M3)

- Explain and try to evaluate how the product may be understood by its target audience. Include precise and detailed examples to support what you are saying. (D3)

Grading tips

To aim for a **merit** grade, your investigation needs to be comprehensive enough to provide you with some detailed information about the target audience. You then need to use this information to start to comment on how the audience is likely to respond to the text and use some detailed examples to support your comments.

To aim for a **distinction** grade, your investigation needs to be wide-ranging and have sufficient depth to allow you to go beyond description and explain in some detail how the audience are likely to respond to the text. The specific examples that you use to justify and support your analysis should be precise and detailed.

PLTS

Planning and carrying out your investigation into the media product and the way the audience responds to it will help you to develop your skills as an **independent enquirer**.

Functional skills

Writing your magazine article will help you to develop your **English** skills in writing.

Freelance copywriter

I work in the advertising industry, helping clients sell more of their products by advertising them to the right people in the right way.

I start by getting to the heart of what a product does and how it can help people. It's useful to put your assumptions aside and look at the product as if for the first time. I then list everything good about the product and the reasons people might have for buying it.

The next stage is to convert these ideas into advertising messages: a slogan. A laptop, for instance, can be advertised with a range of messages, depending on what a customer is looking for. It's also important to use the media most likely to be seen by the customer.

Students, for example, might be sent emails about the low cost of the computer. Mailings through the post might talk to business owners about how easily the laptop integrates with their existing computer system. Press adverts in selected magazines might focus on the laptop's free technical support.

These are examples of advertising that can be targeted to particular people. If the laptop was to be advertised on billboards or on television, and therefore seen by all kinds of people, the message would have to be more general. Here, I would use the idea with the broadest appeal to attract the maximum number of people; something like 'The XYZ laptop. Prepare to be amazed.'

Think about it

1. What areas have you covered in this unit that provide you with the knowledge and skills needed by a freelancer who has to work with lots of different clients and media products? Discuss with your class and then produce a summary of your key points.

2. What processes does a freelance copywriter go through to make sure that they appeal to the right audience?

3. Can the copywriter always ensure that the audience responds in the way that they intended them to?

Just checking

1. What is the difference between a niche market and a mass market?
2. List seven different categories that media producers divide a potential audience into.
3. Why are audience profiles particularly useful to media producers operating within a commercial market?
4. What is the audience measurement panel and how does it work?
5. What are the three key elements that you need to consider when planning the construction of any media product?
6. What does the term 'mode of address' refer to?
7. Why are generic codes and conventions useful to media producers?
8. Name three different types of narrative structure and an audience that each one may appeal to.
9. Identify four organisations that try to regulate the media industry sectors.
10. What does the © symbol stand for?
11. What does the term 'reading a text' mean in this unit?
12. What does the term 'mise-en-scène' refer to?

Assignment tips

- Do lots of your own research into your chosen media industry so that you develop a good understanding of its products and audiences.
- Try to get some practical experience of using all the different audience research techniques. This will make it easier for you to talk about them when you do the assessment activity for LO1.
- When choosing your particular media industry to focus on, think about the work you are doing in your other units so that you can get the right balance.
- Look at a range of different ways in which media products are constructed when undertaking your assessment activity for LO2.
- To aim for a merit grade or better, you need to include examples to illustrate and support what you are saying.
- Check all of your work through before it is finally submitted. Make sure that you have covered all of the required points.

Investigation

The creative media sector is a competitive and dynamic area of British industry, which employs over 500,000 people in a variety of different roles and professions.

Finding out about the different areas of the creative media sector and investigating the products that are produced within it is an important way of improving your knowledge of this broad and diverse sector.

The optional units that you choose to take with your mandatory units allow you to specialise in one or more of the creative media industries. You can choose to look in more detail at video, audio or print production or to explore the developing techniques of interactive media production and computer games development. You can also take a look across the different industries by investigating advertising production and writing for the media, as well as photography and animation.

Whichever optional units you take, you will have to demonstrate your ability to research and investigate the practices, procedures and products within each industry.

Learning outcomes

The table on page 118 shows some of the optional units that contain a learning outcome requiring you to research and investigate an aspect of a particular production industry or the products that it produces. This is usually LO1 in any particular unit, but can sometimes also be LO2 and LO3.

Assessment and grading criteria

Each optional unit shows you what you need to do in order to achieve a **pass**, **merit** or **distinction** grade for the investigation learning outcome. These are all broadly the same and involve you producing a folder of evidence to show that you have investigated and understood the production processes, techniques or technologies, as well as the different elements that make up the media products themselves.

The table below shows you the relevant grading criteria for a sample of the optional units. Further optional units with an investigation element are shown on page 211.

6 Audio production

P1 outline broadcast and non-broadcast audio products and their formats	**M1** describe broadcast and non-broadcast audio products with some detail and with reference to appropriate illustrative examples	**D1** evaluate broadcast and non-broadcast audio products with reference to precise and detailed illustrative examples

7 Print production

P1 outline print production technologies and techniques employed in the industry	**M1** describe print technologies and techniques with some detail and with reference to appropriate illustrative examples	**D1** explain print technologies and techniques with reference to precise and detailed illustrative examples

8 Interactive media production

P1 outline the elements of interactive media production	**M1** describe the elements of interactive media production with some detail and with reference to appropriate illustrative examples	**D1** explain the elements of interactive media production with reference to precise and detailed illustrative examples

10 Animation techniques

P1 outline techniques employed in animation	**M1** describe techniques employed in animation with some detail and with reference to appropriate illustrative examples	**D1** evaluate techniques employed in animation with reference to precise and detailed illustrative examples

11 Web authoring

P1 outline the principles and protocols of web authoring	**M1** describe the principles and protocols of web authoring with some detail and with reference to appropriate illustrative examples	**D1** explain the principles and protocols of web authoring with reference to precise and detailed illustrative examples

How you will be assessed

The investigation element of each of the optional units will be assessed using a number of internal assignments that will be designed and marked by the tutors at your centre. These may be subject to sampling by your centre's External Verifier as part of Edexcel's ongoing quality assurance procedures.

The assignments are designed to allow you to show your understanding of the investigation process, the specific aspects of the production industry you are studying and the products they produce.

Your assessments could be in the form of:

- presentations
- case studies
- practical tasks
- written assignments.

Peter,
Writing for the creative media

I was very interested in print production and was also good at writing. I had talked to my careers advisor and had done some research about how to become a journalist when I am older.

Because of my interest in journalism, I decided to choose Unit 19 Writing for the creative media. I wanted to write for newspapers and magazines so I decided to also take Unit 7 Print production so that I could write my own material for my own printed products.

Both of these optional units had learning outcomes that required me to do some research into the production processes and products. This was very interesting and the best part was when I learned all about the different printing methods and the digital printing techniques that are used today.

I also enjoyed investigating the media products themselves and finding out about the different elements that go into their construction. This helped me in my practical production work as it made me think about the production process more carefully and saved me making a lot of costly mistakes.

- Which optional units have you chosen?
- What are your reasons for choosing these particular ones?
- What skills do you think you will need to develop in order to undertake the investigation parts of them?

Investigation techniques

All of the optional units featured in this section involve you undertaking some form of research as part of your investigation. You will have already learned about some of the main research methods and techniques in Unit 1 and in this section we explore the investigation process in further detail.

Primary research

When investigating your chosen area of media production, you will need to undertake some primary research of your own. In Unit 1, you will have learned about a lot of different primary research methods and you will be able to use some of them here to help you undertake your investigation.

Observation

Observation is a good primary research technique to use for this element of your optional units. You should try to arrange a visit where you are able to observe the production process taking place. This will be easier for some of the production units than others, but it is a good place to start to get an overview of what the production practices and procedures are within a particular industry sector.

Activity: Industry visit

1. Discuss with a class partner which production units you are taking and decide which ones would benefit from a visit to see the production process taking place.
2. Do some research and write down the details of as many relevant companies within your local area as you can.
3. Discuss with your tutor and decide which ones it is worth contacting to see if you can arrange a visit.

What types of company would be useful for you to visit to help you with your research for this unit? When visiting, don't forget to ask if you can take some photographs for your final portfolio.

Interview

If you do manage to arrange a visit to a relevant company then you should also try to include an interview with the owner or with one of the employees. This is another important primary research technique that will help you to understand the industry and its production processes and technology.

Before your visit, you should do some research about the place that you are going to, so that you are prepared and know what sort of questions to ask.

What questions would you like to ask if you have the opportunity to speak to a professional working in your chosen industry sector?

Case study: Visit to a local radio station

Debra was doing Unit 6 Audio production and needed to investigate broadcast and non-broadcast audio products and formats for LO1.

She had already investigated podcasts, Internet radio and in-store audio for the non-broadcast aspects of the unit, but wasn't too sure about the broadcast elements.

Through her tutor, Debra contacted her local BBC radio station and, together with five of her classmates, she was invited to spend an afternoon at the local broadcast studios.

Here she was able to see the different news and feature packages that the station produced and find out about the latest digital audio broadcasting technology that the station was using.

She was also able to see the DJ and the production staff at work and recorded an interview with the station manager.

Debra found this visit to be very useful in improving her knowledge and understanding of radio broadcasting. She was able to include a lot of detailed examples from her visit in her assignment activity for the unit and this helped her gain a distinction grade for the work.

- How did Debra's visit to the radio station help her investigation for Unit 6 Audio production?
- What sort of material would she have hoped to gather while she was there?
- What can you learn from this case study that will be of benefit to your own investigations?

You will also need to explore in some detail the media products that are produced by the industry sector that you have chosen to investigate. One specialist primary research method that can be used to help you undertake this investigation is called **content analysis**.

Key term

Content analysis – the study of the content of a media product. It produces quantifiable data and involves counting particular elements or features within the product.

Content analysis

Content analysis produces quantifiable data and involves counting specific elements or features within a particular media product and then comparing the results with other similar products.

For example, if you are investigating the print industry and its products you may want to see what percentage of a tabloid newspaper like *The Sun* or *The Daily Mirror* is adverts, what percentage is pictures and what percentage is written text. You could then see what the results are for a broadsheet newspaper like *The Times* or *The Guardian* and compare your findings.

You can also use this technique to find out who and what are featured in your media products. For example, how many news stories in a BBC Radio 1 news broadcast feature teenagers, how many feature politicians and how many feature celebrities? How does this compare to a BBC Radio 5 news broadcast on the same day?

Activity: Content analysis

1. Discuss your chosen industry with a class partner and decide which products you would like to undertake a content analysis on.

2. Discuss with your tutor and decide what you would be able to find out about the products from undertaking a content analysis.

3. Plan how you are going to record your results and then undertake your analysis.

4. Write up your results and your conclusions and then discuss your findings with the rest of the class.

Different media products are aimed at different audiences. After you have carried out your content analysis, think about which styles and features you prefer. Are these common in other media products aimed at people of your age or gender?

Secondary research

Secondary research is also an important method that you will use in your investigation. You will need to use the Internet and books to search for relevant information about your chosen production sector. This will be particularly important when you are investigating the different technologies and equipment that are used within the industry.

Hopefully your school or college will have some up-to-date production equipment for you to use for your own production work, but it is also important that you know about the equipment and software that is used within the industry.

You will have already learned about some of the more important websites that you can look at to get information on your chosen media industry and a careful Internet search will provide you with more examples.

As with all secondary research, you will need to carefully select the material that relates directly to your investigation and avoid the temptation to include irrelevant information just for the sake of it.

Think about it

Which primary and secondary research methods are you already familiar with?

Purpose

The purpose of your investigation should be carefully considered before you start to do any detailed research. You need to be clear about what you are trying to find out and the ways that you will attempt to find this information.

Look carefully at the learning outcomes for each of your production units that involve an investigation. Will your research need to improve your knowledge and understanding of the industry, its production techniques, the technology that it uses or the products themselves? Or do you need to find out about all of these aspects?

For example, if you are doing Unit 7 Print production, you need to investigate the techniques and technologies that are used to produce printed material. The main purpose of your investigation will be to find out about the three main techniques that are used:

- printing by hand
- printing using a mechanical process
- printing using new digital techniques.

You will also need to investigate some of the technology that is used with these different processes.

Some of this research can be undertaken by finding out about the different techniques and technologies using the Internet, books and magazines. However, it will be much better if this secondary research is supplemented by the observation of different printing processes through an industrial visit, an interview with a printer and the chance to experience first hand some of the different printing methods.

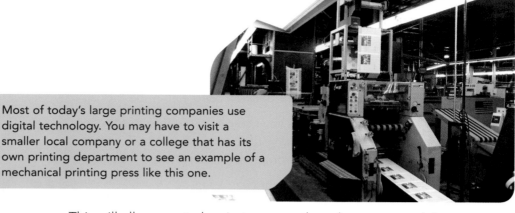

Most of today's large printing companies use digital technology. You may have to visit a smaller local company or a college that has its own printing department to see an example of a mechanical printing press like this one.

This will allow you to begin to assess the advantages and the disadvantages of each method and to have some understanding of the aesthetic and technical issues that a printer has to consider when producing a particular product.

Case study: David, Print production

David's college has its own small printing department and this meant that he was able to have a go at some of the different hand-printing techniques, such as etching, linocut and screen printing. He was able to use the college's photocopier, its laser printer and its inkjet printer to see what the different results were like. He also had the opportunity to investigate the desktop publishing software (DTP) that the college's marketing department used.

All of this allowed David to add some excellent primary research to the initial secondary research that he had done on the Internet. This was a positive start to his investigation into printing techniques and technologies, and he was able to add to this further by visiting a local print company through a contact that his tutor had.

On the visit, David was able to compare an old mechanical press with a new digital press that the company had just bought, and to speak to one of the printers about the differences that this new technology had brought about.

He was also able to see a different software package being used for DTP and talk to one of the designers about the options available.

This information proved to be very useful and David felt more confident in talking about the advantages and disadvantages of the different techniques that he had learned about through his initial research on the Web.

- What different types of research did David undertake?
- Why was this mix of different research methods useful to him?
- What lessons can you learn from this investigation that will help your own?

By contrast, the investigation that you will need to carry out if you are doing Unit 18 Advertising production will be mainly focused on the adverts themselves. The purpose of this investigation will be to:

- examine a number of adverts from a range of different media
- analyse their content
- try to identify the different styles that they have
- try to identify the different persuasive techniques that they use.

The unit does not ask you to find out about the technologies and production processes that are used to make the different types of adverts; instead, you need to look at the way in which the adverts are constructed to try to persuade the audience to buy the product or service they are promoting.

Later on in the advertising unit, you are required to make your own advertisement within a specific medium. You should therefore make sure that the main focus of your investigation into existing advertisements is within the medium of one of your other production units. This will mean that the investigation you carry out for that unit will allow you to make the advert that you plan and design.

For example, the print production unit that you have just looked at will go well with the advertising production unit, as you will already have learned about the print production techniques needed to create a print-based advert.

Celebrity endorsement is an important persuasive technique used within advertising. Do you know any others?

Activity: Persuasive techniques in advertising

1. Gather together a range of different print-based advertisements and look through them to identify a sample of three or four that show persuasive advertising techniques.

2. Cut out the adverts and make a wall display that identifies and explains the different techniques used.

3. Present your display to the rest of the class.

Unit 19 Writing for the creative media requires a similar approach to Unit 18 in that the main purpose of the investigation is to identify and understand the key techniques used in different types of writing for different areas of the media industries.

Unit 8 Interactive media production combines the approaches of Unit 7 and Unit 18 because the purpose of the investigation is to find out about the different elements of interactive media production. This means investigating the different platforms that hold interactive media and the software that is used to produce it, as well as the ways in which text, still and moving images, and sound may be effectively combined in the various types of products.

The iPhone mobile digital device is a popular platform for interactive media products, called applications or apps for short. When developing new apps, producers research the current market and what users want and require. Do some research of your own to find out what apps are currently available.

Case study: Shula, Interactive media production

Shula needed to investigate the different elements that go into making an interactive media product successful.

After first reading about interactive media production in a textbook and doing some research on the Internet into different types of interactive media products, she decided to undertake some primary research of her own.

She devised a questionnaire that asked users of interactive media products about the content of the products, how easy the products were to use, and how attractive the users found the products. The questionnaire also asked them if they knew anything about the techniques that were used to produce the interactive elements.

Shula used the same questionnaire on herself when sampling a range of different interactive media products. This combination of approaches to her investigation allowed her to gain a good understanding of what makes a successful product and what skills she would need to develop when she came to produce her own product.

- What different research techniques did Shula use?
- How did this help her investigation?
- Can you use any of Shula's methods in your investigation?

Presenting your results

The way in which you present the results of your investigation will depend on which format you prefer, or it may be decided by your tutor.

Written report

If you have strong writing skills and want to further develop your ability to present information in written form, then you will probably prefer to present the results of your investigation in the form of a written report.

As with all reports, this should be presented in a logical and well-organised manner and structured in an appropriate way with relevant headings and sub-headings. You might also want to use graphs and charts to represent some of your findings.

You should also try to include some examples of the products that you have studied from the particular industry. This is relatively easy if it is in hard-copy form from the print, advertising or animation industries, but you can also include web-based screen shots to show examples of interactive media and games products, or include scripts and transcriptions from audio products.

Oral presentation

Instead of a written report, you may present your findings in the form of an oral presentation to your tutor and the rest of the class. This can be a good way for you to include some moving image and audio products as examples of the products that you have investigated in your research. It can also help you to develop your speaking and listening skills and improve your confidence when talking in front of a group of people.

If you do present the results of your investigation in this form, then it is important that you make a recording of the presentation so it can be shown to your Internal and External Verifiers. You should also put any additional written material (such as copies of a supporting presentation produced in PowerPoint® presentation graphics program, and relevant material from your primary and secondary research) into an accompanying portfolio.

If you have the choice, would you prefer to present your final results as a written report or an oral presentation? Think about the advantages and disadvantages of each method.

Assessment activity 5.1

The assessment activity that you will undertake for this element of the optional production units will be the investigation into the required aspects of the industry.

The evidence for the achievement of the relevant learning outcome will be the final report – either a written report or an oral presentation – that you produce on the findings of the investigation, together with any supporting material.

This supporting material may include a portfolio of research material gathered during the investigation, together with samples of specific media products that you have investigated and annotated with relevant production and construction information. You may also want to include any relevant witness statements and tutor observations of the investigation being carried out.

Grading tips

To achieve a **merit** grade, your investigation will have to be in some depth. The final report will need to describe in some detail the relevant aspects of the production industry you have investigated and include relevant examples to support the comments that you are making.

To achieve a **distinction** grade, your investigation will need to be fully comprehensive and have sufficient depth to allow you to go beyond simple description in your report. This means you need to explain and justify the comments that you are making and support them with precise and well-developed examples.

PLTS

Undertaking your investigation into your chosen area of creative media production will help you to develop your skills as an **independent enquirer**.

Functional skills

Producing the material for your final report will help you to develop your **English** skills in writing.

Learning outcomes

Unit	Name	Learning outcome
6	Audio production	LO1 know about broadcast and non-broadcast audio products and formats
7	Print production	LO1 know about print production technologies and techniques
8	Interactive media production	LO1 know about the elements of interactive media production
10	Animation techniques	LO1 know about animation techniques
11	Web authoring	LO1 know about web authoring principles and protocols
12	Digital graphics for interactive and print-based media	LO1 know about digital graphics technology
13	2D digital art for computer games	LO1 know about digital graphics technology LO2 know about the graphic styles and graphical themes used in games
14	Deconstructing computer games	LO1 know about computer game platforms LO2 know about computer game components
15	Computer games testing	LO1 know about the game development process LO2 know about the phases of game testing LO3 know about the types of defects that can be found within a game
16	2D computer game engines	LO1 know about 2D game platforms and their limitations LO2 know about the 2D game assets used to build a game world LO3 know how 2D game engines are used to build a game world
17	3D computer game engines	LO1 know about 3D game platforms and their connectable devices LO2 know about the 3D game assets used to build a game world LO3 know how 3D game engines are used to build a game world
18	Advertising production	LO1 know how advertisements are constructed
19	Writing for the creative media	LO1 know about different types of writing produced in the creative media sector
20	Factual production for the creative media	LO1 understand conventions of factual media formats

Think about it

How will you carry out the investigations for your chosen optional units?

As you can see, all but one of the learning outcomes start with the words 'know about' or 'know how', followed by the aspect of the industry and its products that you need to investigate. The final learning outcome in the table starts with the word 'understand', but this is just another way of saying 'know about' or 'know how' and you will still need to investigate the relevant industry practices.

WorkSpace Anita Harrison
Games researcher

While I was at college studying for my National Diploma in Creative Media Production, I secured a placement at a computer games development company.

They were pleased with my work and I was really happy when they offered me a job as a part-time research assistant when I finished the course.

Games development is a fast-paced industry and rival companies are always looking closely at the games market, the players and the products to identify what the next big game is going to be.

Getting ahead of your rivals involves lots of research into what gamers are playing and what their experiences of the games are. Some games have good game play, good graphics and a good narrative, and their reputation just seems to grow. Others simply stink! It is part of my job to find out what will make a game fly and what will make it sink!

A current trend is being able to play a game with friends over the Internet. If it works well, you soon have thousands of people playing the Internet version, long after the initial game has been completed.

I keep up to date with developments by reading articles on the Internet and in specialised magazines. I also try to get my hands on different games so I know what is out there, and I talk to gamers on message boards to see what the current trends are.

It's fun and exciting, but lots of hard work. I have to go into detail to make sure I understand what I am investigating and can communicate it clearly to my boss.

Think about it

1. What skills have you already developed that will help you undertake an effective investigation if you are working for a creative media production company? Discuss with your class and then produce a summary of your key points.

2. What further skills may you need to develop to be successful in this sort of task? Write a list and discuss with the rest of the class.

3. In what ways can an investigation into existing products and production methods lead to innovation and new developments within the creative media sector?

Just checking

1. Which main learning outcome does the investigation element cover?
2. What are the grading criteria for the investigation part of your chosen optional units?
3. Name three types of primary research that are especially useful for the investigation.
4. What is content analysis?
5. Why can an industrial visit be useful to your investigation?
6. What role can secondary research play in your investigation?
7. Should you include all of the material you found from your secondary research in your portfolio?
8. Why is it important to consider the purpose of your investigation before you start any detailed research?
9. What form should the final report on your investigation take?
10. What should you make sure you do if you give an oral presentation?
11. What do you need to include in your report to try to achieve a merit grade?
12. What do you need to do to try to achieve a distinction grade?

Assignment tips

- If your school or college offers you a choice of optional units, choose them carefully so that they reflect your production interests.
- Take some time to look at the learning outcomes for each of the optional production units you have chosen, to see if there are any links that can be made between them.
- Plan your investigations carefully so that you cover all of the required elements.
- Use a combination of different techniques and methods to get all of the information that you need.
- Present your final report with clarity and with confidence.
- Remember to apply the knowledge that you have learned through your investigation to the planning, pre-production and production stages.

Pre-production

Now that you have investigated your chosen areas of the creative media industries it is time to start the process of producing your own product. Media products do not simply appear out of thin air. They all have to be carefully researched and produced, usually by a team of people working together with some form of technology. Their creation follows a logical pattern of pre-production, production and post-production and in the next few chapters we will be looking closely at each of these stages.

Firstly we have pre-production. The starting point for most creative media products is a commission, request, contract or brief from an individual or an organisation who want you to create a product for them. This request will stimulate lots of different ideas, which are explored and considered before a chosen one is put forward as a firm proposal. If your client likes the idea then the proposal is worked on and developed to a point where it is ready to be produced.

This process of developing ideas and preparing the ground for the production to begin is called pre-production; it is a very important stage to get right if you are to produce a successful media product. If your aim is to create a video, audio, print or interactive media product, or a computer game, you will need to undertake a successful pre-production process for your final product to be a success.

Learning outcomes

The table on page 138 shows a sample of the optional units that contain a learning outcome requiring you to undertake a pre-production process. This is usually LO2 in any particular unit, but can sometimes also be LO1, LO3 or elements of LO4.

Assessment and grading criteria

Each optional unit shows you what you need to do in order to achieve a **pass**, **merit** or **distinction** grade for the pre-production related learning outcome. These are all broadly the same and involve you producing a folder of evidence to show the processes that you went through during the pre-production stage.

The table below shows you the relevant grading criteria for a sample of the optional units. Further optional units with a pre-production element are shown on page 214.

5 Video production

| **P1** apply video pre-production techniques to the creation of a video product | **M1** demonstrate competent application of video pre-production techniques to the creation of a video product | **D1** demonstrate skilful application of video pre-production techniques to the creation of a video product |

7 Print production

| **P2** present an idea for printed material which uses an appropriate technology | **M2** present a developed idea for printed material which uses an appropriate technology | **D2** present an imaginative idea for printed material which uses an appropriate technology |

8 Interactive media production

| **P2** present ideas for an interactive media product with reference to format and application | **M2** present developed ideas for an interactive media product with reference to format and application | **D2** present imaginative ideas for an interactive media product with reference to format and application |

9 Photography techniques

| **P1** present an idea for photographic images which shows some relationship to photographic practice | **M1** present a developed idea for photographic images which shows understanding of photographic practice | **D1** present an imaginative idea for photographic images which clearly derives from a good understanding of photographic practice |

10 Animation techniques

| **P2** present an idea for an animation sequence | **M2** present a developed idea for an animation sequence | **D2** present an imaginative idea for an animation sequence |

11 Web authoring

| **P2** plan and present ideas for a website | **M2** present developed ideas for a website | **D2** present imaginative ideas for a website |

12 Digital graphics for interactive and print-based media

| **P2** present ideas for digital graphic images | **M2** present developed ideas for digital graphic images | **D2** present imaginative ideas for digital graphic images |

How you will be assessed

The pre-production element of each of the optional units will be assessed using a number of internal assignments that will be designed and marked by the tutors at your centre. They may be subject to sampling by your centre's External Verifier as part of Edexcel's ongoing quality assurance procedures.

The assignments are designed to allow you to show your understanding of the pre-production processes and your ability to generate and develop your own ideas.

Your assessments will be closely linked to your practical production work and could be in the form of:

- presentations
- case studies
- practical tasks
- pre-production documentation.

Ishmal, Video production

My school needed a promotional DVD that they could show to potential new students and their parents. Some of my classmates and I decided we would form a production team and produce a DVD for the school as our main project for the video production unit.

We all had lots of different ideas for what we should do, so we wrote them all down and talked them through. This was a good process to go through and it got everybody's brains buzzing. We explored a few of the favourite ideas a little further before working up one idea into a firm proposal, which we pitched to the deputy head. She really liked the idea and asked us to go ahead and produce it.

This was really scary as now we had a real project that would be shown to hundreds of people! The pressure was on to get the production right and so we were really pleased that we had to go through a pre-production stage.

Some people in the team were impatient and just wanted to start filming, but we soon realised that this simply would not have worked and we were all very glad that we had the time to plan and prepare things properly. It really did make a difference and the production stage ran so much more smoothly than some of our earlier projects had done.

- Why do you think a pre-production stage is so important?
- What sort of things do you need to do in the pre-production stage?
- What skills do you think you will be able to develop through this important stage?

Pre-production skills

All of the optional units will involve you and your team going through a process of pre-production before the actual production stage begins. This section concentrates on the things you will need to do and think about in preparation for production.

Generating ideas

Creative production starts with creative thinking, so getting your brains engaged and your ideas flowing is an important first step in the pre-production process.

Most of your practical production work is likely to be carried out in groups and so a good way of starting to generate ideas for your product is to sit round a table and discuss a variety of suggestions.

It is important that everybody in your group makes a contribution to the discussion and that all of the ideas are recorded in some way so that they don't become lost or forgotten.

You can use a flip-chart or whiteboard to write down the ideas as they are discussed, or you may want to record the session so that you have evidence of the process taking place.

Think about it

Why does the creative media sector demand so many new ideas for its creative products?

This stage of the pre-production process is all about putting ideas on the table, no matter how strange they may at first appear. Why is it important that all possible options are considered?

Running a meeting

You need to get your group working together effectively and you also need to gather evidence for your final portfolio, showing how you worked together as a successful production team.

This will require regular team meetings and so, in the pre-production stage, it is important to get your team meetings established and off to a good start.

To be effective, meetings need to be well–structured and the best way of doing this is to have an **agenda**. This is a list of the items that are to be covered in the meeting, which is sent to people before the meeting starts so that they know what it is going to be about and have time to prepare.

It is common practice to have an **AOB** (**a**ny **o**ther **b**usiness) item at the end of the meeting so that any member of the team can raise additional points or issues not covered in the original agenda.

It is important that a record of the meeting is produced, containing a brief summary of the points discussed and the actions that people have agreed to undertake. These are called the **minutes** of the meeting – see chapter 2 (Unit 2), Communication techniques for creative media production, page 45 – and are usually discussed at the start of the next meeting to make sure they are a true and accurate record of what was said.

Key terms

Agenda – a list of the items that are to be covered in a specific meeting, together with the date, time and location of the meeting.

AOB – agenda item that stands for 'any other business'.

 Remember

Writing minutes is a skilled task. Don't make the mistake of trying to write down everything that was said. Try instead to listen carefully to what is being said and then summarise the key points and actions.

Meeting to discuss video production

Date	17 October 2010
Time	2.30 p.m.
Location	Room 2A

Agenda

1. Decide what roles we need in the team
2. Assign roles to each person
3. Discuss story ideas
4. Ideas for locations
5. Any other business

Date: 05.03.11   **Time:** 9.30 a.m.   **Place:** Room 57
Present: John, Sarah, Paul, Kieran
Apologies: Sasha   **Minutes taken by:** Sarah

Minutes:

1. Job roles discussed and allocated: John to be cameraman, Sarah to be director, Paul to be editor. Kieran and Sasha will both be acting and providing production support.
2. Paperwork outstanding: John and Paul have already produced the script and storyboards but some final planning documents are still outstanding – these are to be produced as follows:
   - Sarah and Kieran – location recce and risk assessments
   - Sasha and Paul – call sheets
   - All group members – work on altering production schedule as timescales have changed due to bad weather.
3. Possible filming dates discussed: suggested 25–28 March for all filming at all locations.

Points for next meeting:

1. Assess progress made on production.
2. Check through all paperwork.
3. Discuss contingency plans prior to filming.

Date of Next Meeting: 19 March 2011

Figure 6.1 (above): An agenda should be concise and include details of the date, time and location of the meeting. Why are these features important?

Figure 6.2 (right): Team meeting minutes show who was present and who gave their apologies. Why do you think this is important?

Choosing one idea

Generating ideas is one thing, but at the end of the process you will need to decide on one idea to take forward and develop into a **proposal**. This is a document that explains your idea to a potential client or customer. Your early discussion meetings should produce a range of different ideas. The whole group needs to discuss the advantages and disadvantages of each idea and whittle the list down to a favourite chosen idea.

When looking at each idea in turn, it may be easy to reject those that are perhaps too ambitious for the timescale that you have, too expensive to produce or simply too dangerous.

You may be able to reduce the initial list to two or three ideas that you need to consider in more detail. A **SWOT analysis** can help you with this process. This involves the team discussing each idea and, for each one, identifying the:

* **s**trengths
* **w**eaknesses
* **o**pportunities
* **t**hreats (or barriers).

Key terms

Proposal – a document that explains your idea to a potential client or customer.

SWOT analysis – a simple tool to assess the strengths and weaknesses of an idea, as well as the opportunities that it will bring and the potential threats.

Strengths	Weaknesses
Display range of creative skills	Too big a project? Hard to coordinate and manage
Good team project	One weak element might pull everybody down
Involve lots of different elements (written text, photos, video, sound)	College already has a website
Low cost to produce	Some members of team have poor IT skills
Achievable in time-scale	
High profile project	
Opportunities	**Threats**
Real client: Head of Marketing	Client is a busy man!
Apple Mac suite	Resources are heavily used by other learners and might not be available when we want them
Digital cameras (video and still)	
Digital sound recording equipment	Needs to be completed by end of April
Media Technician has web experience	

Figure 6.3: SWOT analysis. Using these four simple headings can help you to decide which of your ideas is best. How has SWOT analysis helped you to assess your own ideas?

Activity: SWOT analysis

1. Choose your three best ideas.

2. Write the name of each idea on a separate piece of paper and then draw a large + sign in the middle of each piece of paper to divide it into four sections.

3. In the top left section write the word *Strengths*, in the top right write the word *Weaknesses*, in the bottom left write the word *Opportunities* and in the bottom right put the word *Threats*.

4. For each of your ideas, undertake a SWOT analysis by discussing the strengths and weaknesses of each idea, the opportunities that it will bring and the potential barriers that may get in your way of doing it. Write a summary of your findings in the relevant sections of the paper.

5. At the end of the process, decide on which idea is the best one to take forward.

Developing your idea

Having decided on the best idea to take forward, you now have to work this idea into a firm proposal. This will involve a range of different skills and techniques, some of which will be the same regardless of which optional production units you are doing and some of which will vary depending on which production medium you are working in.

Research

During your investigation work in the previous chapter, you will have used a range of the research methods and techniques that you learned about in Unit 1. Here, there is an opportunity for you to develop your research skills to help you gather information to develop your ideas further, whichever optional unit you are undertaking. You will want to use a range of these methods and techniques to find out more about your potential audience and about existing products that are similar to the one that you are proposing to make.

If you are making a video product then a specific primary research technique you will want to use is a **recce**. This is a visit to a potential location to check out its suitability for filming. While undertaking the recce, you can also look at potential **health and safety issues**: this will help you later on in the production process when you will have to undertake a **risk assessment**.

Key term

Recce – a visit to a potential location to check out its suitability for recording your product.

Case study: Carrying out a recce

An independent production company, New Age Productions, was given the brief of producing a video for young people warning about the dangers of drinking alcohol. During the pre-production stage they did some test shots in the studio but it looked too false, so they decided to explore the idea of filming most of it on location.

This involved doing a recce in their local city to find suitable locations. This proved to be a really useful part of their pre-production work and they got some great ideas for shots by visiting potential places to film. They also managed to interview some bar owners while on the recce and found one who was happy for the footage to be filmed in her bar. This made the video look more realistic and they were careful not to show the bar in a negative way.

- If you were to film a video about the dangers of alcohol to young people, what locations would you check out in your town or city?

- Can you think of any specific problems or barriers that you may face trying to film such a video?

- Why was the company careful to not show the bar in a negative way?

If you were a professional location scout, how would you go about researching for suitable filming locations?

Activity: Links with Unit 1

1. Look at the work that you have already undertaken in Unit 1. See whether there are any links to the research work that you will be doing in this unit.

2. Write down a list of the potential research methods and techniques that you may want to use.

Permissions

When you are developing your ideas, you will need to think about any **permissions** that you will need to get before the production process can begin. This may include such things as:

- finding out who owns the copyright to a particular piece of music or a logo and how much it will cost for you to be able to use it in your production

- getting permission from the owner of a location to film there

- getting permission from the people who will be in a scene that you are planning to film or a photograph that you are going to take.

Case study: Filming in London

London is the third busiest city in the world for filming and there is a film or television crew on the streets almost every day of the year.

Film London is an important source of information for crews wanting to film in the capital. Its website contains information on the permissions that are needed and the organisations that need to be contacted.

In 2007, Film London provided information and advice to 647 productions that filmed in the capital. Of the productions assisted:

- 40% were television projects
- 21% were features
- 18% were commercials or promotions
- 14% were corporate and stills shoots
- 7% were short films.

To obtain a link to the Film London website, please see the Hotlinks section on page ii.

- **Visit the Film London website to find out more information about the permissions that are needed before a crew can start filming in London.**

- **What sort of things do the permissions cover?**

- **What permissions would you need to film in your nearest town or city? You will need to do some research of your own to answer this question.**

Getting people's permission for them to be in your product can save a lot of problems later on. Why do you think permissions are important?

Think about it

What problems might you face if you used some material in your media product that broke the copyright laws?

Equipment

Any media production will involve the use of some form of equipment to record, edit and manipulate your raw material into the finished product. Video, audio and photographic products will need equipment to record and capture the sounds and images that you need. Computer hardware and software is now at the heart of the editing, origination and production processes that are used to complete all digital media products.

When developing your ideas, you need to be aware of what equipment and resources you will have available to you. You may have a really good idea for an aerial shot swooping over a city landscape, but if you haven't got a crane or a helicopter then you may have trouble filming it!

Test shoots and recordings

For the video, photography and audio production units, you will want to do some test shoots and recordings to help you to develop your idea further. These can help you to decide what elements you will be able to include in your final product and what the best way is to get the effect that you want.

For example, for a sound production project you may need to find a suitable location for an audio recording. You may have an idea to record a country scene in the local park, but after doing a test recording in the location you may discover that the traffic noise is too loud and want to use a quieter location instead.

Activity: Test shoots and recordings

1. If your project involves photography, or video or audio recording, write down a list of the test shoots or recordings that may help you to further develop your ideas and test out if your ideas will work.

2. Plan what you will need to do to undertake the test shoots/recordings and discuss further with your tutor.

Checking whether or not you can actually get the shot that you have in your head is an important part of the pre-production process. What problems may you encounter at this stage?

Pre-production paperwork

The pre-production paperwork that you will develop will vary depending on which production medium you are working in, and will form an important part of your completed portfolio.

For example, if you are planning a video production, you will develop and refine your ideas through a storyboard and script. For a printed product, such as a magazine or newspaper, you will produce ideas sheets, rough drafts, concept drawings and thumbnails of the pages you are planning to produce. For an interactive media product, you may use all of the above together with a mood board to give you an idea about the overall look and feel of the product. A web-based interactive product may also need a structure diagram to show the links between the different web pages and the order in which they are accessed by the user.

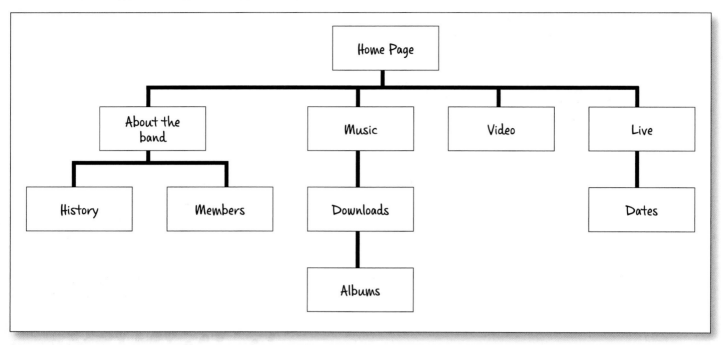

Figure 6.4: A structure diagram allows you to plan the order and structure of the web pages for an interactive product. Here is an example that a learner produced for a website about a band. What would you include in a structure diagram for a website that you are producing?

Figure 6.5: Thumbnails are rough sketches of the proposed page layout. Here is one that was used in the design of this book (see p. 4). Can you see how the different elements are shown? Does this thumbnail look like the real thing?

Some pre-production paperwork is common to all forms of creative media production. We have already mentioned the need to undertake risk assessments and to have considered the relevant health and safety issues and there is more information about this in the next chapter.

As your plans come together, and before you start the production process, you will need to put together a detailed production schedule showing what you are going to do and when and how you are going to do it. This schedule is your plan that you will take with you through to the production stage. It will help you to keep track of where you are and what you need to do.

Table 6.1 lists examples of the pre-production paperwork you should use for each type of product, together with an explanation of what each one is. The next page shows two examples of pre-production paperwork used by some Creative Media Production learners.

Table 6.1: Pre-production paperwork. What paperwork will you need to produce for your production?

Production type	Pre-production paperwork	What is it?
All types of production	Production schedule	A detailed plan of how and when your production will take place
	Risk assessment	Details of potential things that could go wrong and relevant health and safety issues (see Production, pages 146–149, for more information)
	Contingency plan	Links to your risk assessment and shows what your alternative plan is if some of the things that could go wrong actually happen
	Permissions	Forms that give you permission to film in the places that you want and include the people that you want in your final product
Video	Storyboard	A visualisation of each shot of your finished programme that includes timings and details of the soundtrack
	Script	What the people in the programme are going to say, together with how they are going to say it and any music or sound effects
	Shooting script	A more detailed script that includes camera angles, locations, types of shot, dialogue and soundtrack
Audio	Script	What the people in the programme are going to say, together with how they are going to say it and any music or sound effects
Print and interactive media	Concept drawings	Drawings of how a picture or page may look
	Thumbnails	Rough sketches of a proposed page layout
	Mood boards	Collections of different examples of colour, text and styles to show how the finished product will look and feel
Web-based interactive media	Structure diagrams	Like a storyboard for a web-based interactive product that shows the hierarchy of the pages and the links between them
Animation	Concept drawings	Drawings of how the characters and backgrounds may look
	Storyboard	A visualisation of each sequence of your finished animation that includes timings, animation techniques and details of the soundtrack
	Script	What the people in the animation are going to say, together with how they are going to say it and any music or sound effects

Here are some examples of the types of pre-production paperwork that you should be using.

Storyboard

Figure 6.6: Storyboards provide camera operators with a visual representation of what they should shoot. What other information should you add to this storyboard?

Audio script

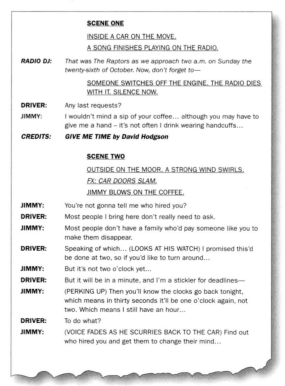

Figure 6.7: This audio script is for a radio play. As well as containing the actors' lines, what other information does it show?

Proposal

After you have developed your idea and completed your initial pre-production paperwork, you are ready to write up the final proposal and then present your idea.

The proposal is usually a written document in which you sell your idea to a potential client or customer. In the proposal, you need to explain very clearly to the person reading it:

- what your idea is
- who the target audience is
- what purpose your product has.

You should also include some information about:

- the equipment you are going to use
- who is in the team
- what the costs are going to be
- what the timescale of the production is.

This all needs to be communicated in a clear and positive way so that after reading the proposal the client, customer or tutor thinks 'Yes! What a great idea. Let's go ahead with it.'

Checklist for a proposal:

- Remember that the person reading it may not have any other information about you or your proposed product and this is your one chance to impress them.
- Explain very clearly what your proposed product is.
- Explain what the purpose of your product is.
- Identify the target audience.
- Describe briefly the research that you have undertaken.
- Identify who is in your production team.
- List the equipment that you are going to use.
- Describe briefly how you are going to produce your proposed product.
- Give some indication of the costs and any revenue you will generate from sales of the product or from advertising or sponsorship.
- Say when the product will be completed by.
- Check that your language is clear and accurate, and that you have used the correct media terms.

Activity: Proposal

1. Use the checklist to produce a draft proposal for one of the products that you are planning to make in one of your optional production units.

2. Discuss your draft with the rest of your production group and then show it to your tutor.

3. Listen carefully to their feedback and then produce a finished version of your proposal.

Presenting your ideas

You will need to present your ideas to your client; this is often called a **pitch** – see chapter 2 (Unit 2), Communication techniques for creative media production, page 37. Most of the production units require you to pitch your proposal to your client (if you have one) or to your tutor and the rest of your class.

The pitch is often used in the creative media industries to support what is said in the proposal. It is the main way in which a media producer can communicate their ideas to a potential client or customer face to face.

Remember

You have already learned the importance of effective communication skills and how to deliver a successful presentation in Units 1 and 2. A pitch is a type of presentation that uses a range of communication skills, so you should look back to the first two units to help you prepare and deliver a successful pitch.

A successful pitch can make the difference between a product being taken up or rejected; therefore, getting the pitch right is an important skill to learn. What do you think makes a successful pitch?

Activity: Pitching your ideas

1. Read through the sections on delivering a presentation in Unit 1 and effective communication skills in Unit 2.

2. With your production group, plan a pitch for your proposed product.

3. Make sure that you cover in the pitch all of the elements that you have put in your written proposal.

4. Think about any additional things that may go in your pitch. Because it is a presentation you can include slides produced in PowerPoint® presentation graphics program. You can also show the client examples of your pre-production work to support what you are saying.

5. Think about any questions you may want to ask your client in your pitch.

6. Arrange for the pitch to be recorded.

7. Deliver your pitch to the client, customers or tutor and classmates.

8. Watch the recording of the pitch and listen to the feedback from your client, customers, tutor and classmates.

9. Review how the pitch went and identify any ways in which it could have been improved.

BTEC Assessment activity 6.1

The assessment activity for this element of the optional production units will be the pre-production work that you undertake.

The evidence for the achievement of the relevant learning outcome will be:

- the pre-production documentation and paperwork that you complete
- the minutes of your pre-production meetings
- your final written proposal
- the recording and related paperwork from your pitch.

All of this material should be carefully structured and organised in a portfolio together with the related production and post-production work. You may also want to include any relevant witness statements and tutor observations of the pre-production work being carried out.

Grading tips

To achieve a **merit** grade, your pre-production work must be well developed and well organised. It must demonstrate some depth and detail, as well as the ability to work carefully and competently.

To achieve a **distinction** grade, your pre-production work must be imaginative, thorough and well detailed. It must also demonstrate a high degree of detailed application.

PLTS

Undertaking your pre-production work in your chosen area of creative media production will help you to develop your skills as a **creative thinker**.

Functional skills

Presenting your pitch will help you to develop your **English** skills in speaking and listening.

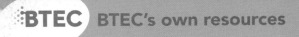

Learning outcomes

Unit	Name	Learning outcome
5	Video production	LO1 be able to carry out pre-production for a proposed video product
7	Print production	LO2 be able to develop ideas for printed material
8	Interactive media production	LO2 be able to develop ideas for an interactive media product
9	Photography techniques	LO1 be able to generate ideas for photographic images informed by photographic practice
10	Animation techniques	LO2 be able to develop ideas for an animation sequence
11	Web authoring	LO2 be able to develop a plan for a website
12	Digital graphics for interactive and print-based media	LO2 be able to generate ideas for digital graphic images
13	2D digital art for computer games	LO3 be able to use pencil to draw concept art for a game
16	2D computer game engines	LO4 be able to build a 2D game world to a specification
17	3D computer game engines	LO4 be able to build a 3D game world to a specification
18	Advertising production	LO2 be able to develop ideas for an advertisement
19	Writing for the creative media	LO2 be able to generate ideas for written material
20	Factual production for the creative media	LO2 be able to generate ideas for a factual media product
21	Creative media production project	LO1 be able to prepare a proposal for a media product LO2 be able to complete pre-production for a proposed media product

Adhika Desai
Production assistant in interactive media

I work for an interactive media company, so my role as a production assistant (PA) is very varied. It involves me with all stages of the production process, but, because I am relatively new, most of my time at the moment is spent in pre-production.

Here I have to work closely with other members of the team and get involved with lots of different aspects. Being a PA means having technical, creative and administrative skills and knowledge, and also being a good people person.

I also have to be very organised, as the pace of change when we are developing a new product can be very fast. I work closely with designers, writers and producers and have to listen carefully to what they want me to do and what information they need next. I also have to keep the pre-production paperwork and documentation well organised, as they often ask me for the latest version of a storyboard or script so that some changes can be made.

In my time here, I have learned that having a positive attitude and a 'can do' approach are both important to working in the industry. I have also discovered that you have to be able to work well on your own, as well as being an effective team member.

Think about it

1. What skills do you have already that will help you to play a positive role in a pre-production team? Discuss with the rest of your class and then produce a written summary of your key points.
2. What further skills may you need to develop to be successful in this sort of area? Write a list and discuss with the rest of the class.
3. Why is pre-production such an important stage of the creative media production process?

Just checking

1. What are the grading criteria for the pre-production part of your chosen optional units?
2. What is a good way to start generating ideas for a new product?
3. What items should be included on a meeting agenda?
4. What does AOB stand for?
5. Should the minutes of a meeting include every single word that was spoken?
6. What is a SWOT analysis?
7. What pre-production paperwork should you use for your chosen area?
8. What is a proposal?
9. What elements should a proposal include?
10. What is a pitch?
11. What skills do you need to deliver a successful pitch?

Assignment tips

- Issue an agenda for your production group meetings a few days before the date of the meeting, so people know the time, date, location and what is going to be discussed.
- Always have an AOB at the end, so people can raise any additional points.
- Make sure each meeting is minuted, so people know what was said and you have some good evidence of pre-production work and teamwork for your final portfolio.
- Use a SWOT analysis to help choose the best idea.
- Spend time planning your production and use the correct pre-production paperwork to help you develop your ideas.
- Use a clear, logical structure when writing your proposal. Make sure that you check your spelling and punctuation and that you have used the correct words.
- Practise your pitch before you deliver it so that you can make any improvements before the big day.

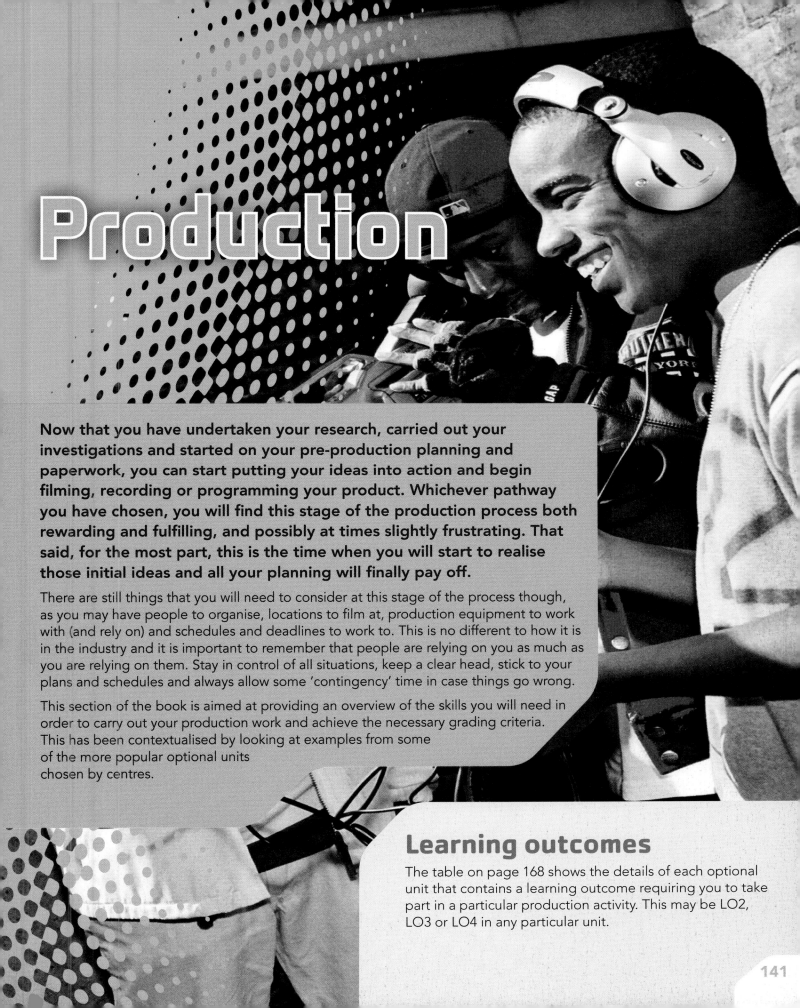

Production

Now that you have undertaken your research, carried out your investigations and started on your pre-production planning and paperwork, you can start putting your ideas into action and begin filming, recording or programming your product. Whichever pathway you have chosen, you will find this stage of the production process both rewarding and fulfilling, and possibly at times slightly frustrating. That said, for the most part, this is the time when you will start to realise those initial ideas and all your planning will finally pay off.

There are still things that you will need to consider at this stage of the process though, as you may have people to organise, locations to film at, production equipment to work with (and rely on) and schedules and deadlines to work to. This is no different to how it is in the industry and it is important to remember that people are relying on you as much as you are relying on them. Stay in control of all situations, keep a clear head, stick to your plans and schedules and always allow some 'contingency' time in case things go wrong.

This section of the book is aimed at providing an overview of the skills you will need in order to carry out your production work and achieve the necessary grading criteria. This has been contextualised by looking at examples from some of the more popular optional units chosen by centres.

Learning outcomes

The table on page 168 shows the details of each optional unit that contains a learning outcome requiring you to take part in a particular production activity. This may be LO2, LO3 or LO4 in any particular unit.

Assessment and grading criteria

Each optional unit shows you what you need to do in order to achieve a **pass**, **merit** or **distinction** grade for the production related learning outcome. These are all broadly the same and involve you producing a folder of evidence to show the processes that you went through during the production stage.

The table below shows you the relevant grading criteria for a sample of the optional units. Further optional units with a production element are shown on page 216.

5 Video production

P2 undertake a technical role in the creation of a video product	**M2** competently carry out a technical role in the creation of a video product	**D2** skilfully carry out a technical role in the creation of a video product

6 Audio production

P2 use audio technology to create an audio product that partially realises intentions	**M2** use audio technology competently to create an audio product that mainly realises intentions	**D2** use audio technology skilfully to create an audio product that clearly realises intentions

7 Print production

P3 use print technology and techniques to create a print product that partially realises intentions	**M3** use print technology and techniques competently to create a print product that mainly realises intentions	**D3** use print technology and techniques skilfully to create a print product which clearly realises intentions

8 Interactive media production

P3 use interactive media technology to create an interactive media product that partially realises intentions	**M3** use interactive media technology competently to create an interactive media product that mainly realises intentions	**D3** use interactive media technology skilfully to create an interactive media product that clearly realises intentions

9 Photography techniques

P2 use photographic technology to create photographs that partially realise intentions	**M2** use photographic technology competently to create photographs that mainly realise intentions	**D2** use photographic technology skilfully to create photographs which clearly achieve intentions

10 Animation techniques

P3 use animation techniques to create an animation sequence that partially realises intentions	**M3** use animation techniques competently to create an animation sequence that mainly realises intentions	**D3** use animation techniques skilfully to create an animation sequence that clearly realises intentions

How you will be assessed

As you can see, there are many production units within the BTEC First in Creative Media Production, but not all of them will be covered on your programme of study.

For each production unit, you will be required to produce a final product that fits the conventions of your chosen medium. Your product will be assessed by your tutor for its overall quality, relevance and fitness for purpose. Work submitted may be subject to sampling by your centre's External Verifier as part of Edexcel's ongoing quality assurance procedures.

Your assessment could be in the form of:

- tutor observations
- learner-generated production paperwork
- production logs or journals
- the completed final product.

Georgia, Print production

I am interested in becoming a journalist after I have finished my studies and felt it was important for me to understand the print production process so that I knew how my written work would look in the end.

I really enjoyed the written side of this unit and was pleased with the copy I had produced, writing a review of a local band. While I found this process enjoyable, I was surprised at how much I also enjoyed putting my print product together. At my college, we used a digital software package that allowed us to import pictures we had taken ourselves with digital cameras. It also provided different layouts for us so that we could choose what style we wanted for our backgrounds.

For my piece, I imported images from the Internet, as I couldn't always get the right images using my camera; I wanted some lively scenes from rock concerts and well-known bands for my front cover, so I had to look elsewhere for them. I spent a lot of time cropping and trimming the images to fit my layout and adding titles and captions to add meaning to my work. I was really pleased with the final product and proud that I had done it all myself.

I still want to be a journalist because I love going out and finding a story, meeting people and writing up my work so that it will appeal to the reader. However, I wouldn't completely rule out print production work in the future; it was great fun and I learned a lot!

- How has Georgia drawn together production skills from a range of media?
- What do you think are the challenges in production work?
- How will you develop your skills?

Stages in production

Whether you choose video, audio, print or digital media production there are certain processes that you need to go through in order to produce your products. This section concentrates on different production processes and how to implement the paperwork you will have produced during the pre-production phase of your work. We will look at:

- health and safety

- assigning individual roles, as you will most likely be working in a group situation

- carrying out the responsibilities related to each role.

Finally, we will look at recording footage and creating layouts, as well as reviewing your work prior to moving on to post-production. Not all of these phases are relevant to each process; for example, you will only really record footage in video and audio production and creating layouts is specific to print productions and written formats. Similarly, you will need to review recorded footage before proceeding to post-production, whereas other areas, such as creating a website, will involve an ongoing process of checks and reviews.

Group roles and responsibilities

During pre-production, all members of the group should have been allocated a role or responsibility either as cast or crew for your chosen production. In professional productions, these people would already be employed by the company and most roles would be carried out by separate individuals. In your case, you are likely to have to take on more than one role, and that may be in front of the camera or microphone as well as behind it!

The best way of deciding on group roles is to play on individual strengths and ensure that people are comfortable with the roles and responsibilities they have been given. Here is an activity that will help you with these decisions and give you an idea of the responsibilities included with each of these roles.

Think about it

There are many specialised job roles in the creative media sector. Can you name some that are relevant to your own production process?

Activity: Identifying and allocating roles in video production

Below is a list of possible roles that will need to be taken on by members of your group. Make a note of the main responsibilities and outline the skills that a person will require to undertake each production role.

Director – in charge of the overall aesthetic of the product (how your production looks on camera), ensuring that the script and storyboard is 'visualised' correctly.

Camera operator – films the footage and works closely with the director. They will need to set up the camera and tripod, do white balance (where necessary) and ensure that they have sufficient tape and battery life for filming. They will also have to ensure equipment is in good working order.

Props supervisor – props are all the objects that are required during filming to make sets and scenes more realistic. The person in charge of this area will have to source and provide all the props necessary for filming and ensure that they are available, in good condition, as and when needed.

Actors – will obviously appear in your production and will need to be reliable individuals who will turn up on set when required, listen to the director and be prepared to repeat scenes as and when required.

There are only a limited number of roles here as you are undertaking small productions at this stage and it is important not to overload people with too many responsibilities at one time. Unlike professional productions, in this case it will be the role of the director and not the producer to organise things, making sure everything is where it should be at any given time.

What are the potential problems that you may encounter on location with your cast and crew? How will you overcome them?

The above activity is just an illustrative example and can be used as guidance if you are working on different pathways. If you have chosen audio production, you will still have similar cast and crew allocations as you will need people to appear in the programme as well as record it. It may be that you will work in smaller teams as there is a bit less equipment involved and less likelihood of location work.

Interactive and print media learners are more likely to work alone, but can also form small production teams. For example, if you decide to work on a school newspaper you will need journalists and editors, as well as printers and layout designers. In these circumstances, you can possibly work on two units at the same time, such as Unit 7 Print production and Unit 20 Factual production for the creative media.

If you're working as a team, how will you divide the roles out?

Health and safety

Ensuring that you understand the standard health and safety practices used within the creative media industries is an essential part of all practical production work.

During your studies, you will be using various pieces of technical equipment both in the classroom and outside of the school or college premises, therefore, it is essential that you understand how to operate it correctly and, of course, safely. In addition to the equipment, you will also need to ensure that you keep yourself safe, minimising any risks to your own personal safety and the safety of those around you.

One of the most important things to remember is that there are places and situations you may encounter that could be potentially hazardous to you and those around you. Some hazards you may experience include:

- tripping hazards
- adverse weather conditions
- unsafe working environments
- working with electrical equipment

Think about it

Following correct health and safety procedures will mean that your productions will run smoothly and you will avoid unnecessary setbacks. There are some famous cases where media producers have failed to take the necessary safety precautions with dire consequences – can you think of any?

- working with or around the public
- working on location.

It is important, before you start a production, to carefully assess any potential hazards and how to deal with them. The best way to do this is by using some form of **risk assessment** documentation, a copy of which has been provided for you in the activity on page 148. This form must contain:

- details and the title of the production
- the names of everyone involved in the production
- the production location
- the date the risk assessment took place.

After you have provided this information, you should fill out a table that locates and assesses the potential hazards and how they can be dealt with. This table should include:

- identification of each potential hazard
- hazard ratings (for example, high – 5 and low – 0)
- an outline of how each hazard can be reduced or avoided
- details of who is to take responsibility for reducing hazards and when these actions should be completed by.

It is also beneficial to do an evaluation of the risk assessment you have carried out to ensure that you have identified all potential hazards and fully considered how they can be overcome.

Failure to assess potential risks can have serious consequences. What risks and hazards may be involved in your media production work?

Activity: Identifying potential hazards

Being able to identify potential hazards and how to avoid them is extremely important. Look at the chart below outlining some of the activities you may undertake during your production work. One hazard and solution has already been identified for each activity, can you think of any more?

Activity	Hazard #1	Hazard #2	Solution #1	Solution #2
Using computer software packages to create/edit production work	Eye strain as a result of looking at the screen for extended periods of time		Take regular breaks away from the screen to rest the eyes	
Filming using a mains power supply in busy corridor	Power cable is a potential tripping hazard		Keep cabling secured using tape or crew members to ensure it doesn't get under the feet of crew or passers by	
Transporting production equipment to a location	Lifting heavy equipment		Ensure crew members transporting equipment bend and lift correctly to avoid injury	

Now discuss your results with the other members of your crew or class. Have they identified the same hazards and solutions as you or have they identified things that you haven't and vice versa? Can you think of any other activities that may have potential hazards?

Now try making your own risk assessment chart or copy and fill in the one provided below, which is similar to those used in the industry.

Production title:	Skater Boy
Date:	27 January 2009
Task:	Film action footage
Location:	Green Lane Skate park
Personnel	Director, actors, camera operator, crew

Name:	Role:
Natasha	Director
Lewis	Actor – lead male
Paulina	Actor – lead female
Mike	Camera operator
Tom	Props and general assistant

Potential hazard	Risk rating (0 = no risk 5 = high risk)	How can risk be managed and who is responsible?
Adverse weather – rain or ice	5	As November is a cold month, the risk of bad weather is high. Cameras will need to be protected from rain – camera operator. Personnel need to watch their footing if surfaces are slippery – all cast and crew.
Actor falling off skateboard	4	Action shots could prove dangerous, falls on the skate ramp could cause injury – actor to wear protective clothing and pads.
Falling debris from trees	3	If windy twigs etc. could fall from trees – camera operator and director to ensure crew work in safe areas to avoid this.
Uneven ground	2	The skate park is slightly rutted in places due to constant use – camera operator to take care when filming handheld and tracking shots.

Activity: Amerdeep's directorial debut

Amerdeep has been given a production brief that requires him to obtain video footage of his school football team playing in the semi-finals. He has been asked to make sure that all members of the team are seen on camera and he has to mix action shots and team interviews in his final piece.

As Amerdeep will be filming inside and outside there will be different hazards depending on the working environment.

Amerdeep is busy drawing up the script and storyboard, so he has asked you to carry out a risk assessment for him. He has asked you to assess the locations listed below.

1. The school football field, which has already been used for a number of matches this year and so is quite rutted. It is mid November, what are the potential hazards for the crew and spectators?

2. The school changing rooms. The school is an older building and the changing rooms are quite small and cramped with little space around the benches, which are in the middle of the room. Amerdeep wants to do post-match interviews in here, is this viable? Outline and explain your reasons.

3. The head teacher's office. The head teacher has been asked to say a few words about the team's recent successes. The office has a south-facing window and the head teacher likes to have the heating on, so the office, whilst being very bright, is often hot and not very well ventilated. How suitable is this working environment for your film crew? What can be done to improve working conditions?

PLTS

Analysing and evaluating information, judging its relevance and values when developing an understanding of the requirements of the planning and pre-production phase and the use of appropriate paperwork for a production, will help you to develop your skills as an **independent enquirer**.

Functional skills

Reviewing use of capture software and storage facilities will help you to improve your **ICT** skills.

The preceding sections have outlined for you some of the common elements of the production process. For most productions, you will be required to work in a group, cooperating and sharing ideas with others. Similarly, health and safety is of great importance to all areas of production, as it ensures safe working practices are being maintained at all times.

All the various production processes will now begin to differ and the capturing of footage or creation of a product can begin. All of the planning and paperwork that you have put in place will help your productions run smoothly. The following sections offer a range of production practices, which provide illustrative examples of the work you may undertake.

Video production
Paperwork

Before undertaking your filming, you should have issued a **call sheet** (see Figure 7.1 below) to all of the members of the crew so they are aware of where they need to be and what equipment and props are required on location at that time. Below is a copy of a call sheet that has been filled in to give you an idea of what it should look like.

The other paperwork that you should have on set with you is:

- copies of your script for the actors
- storyboards for the camera operators and crew (see page 134 for an example).

Copies of these documents should have been issued after completion during the pre-production process, therefore the cast and crew should already be extremely familiar with the content. Before filming, your cast should be well rehearsed as it is essential that you don't waste valuable filming time waiting around for people to get their lines right.

Group members should bring a copy of the documents relevant to their roles with them on location. That said, there is always a possibility that someone will forget a copy so it is advisable to always carry spare documents to location shoots just in case.

Production title: **Skater Boy** Sheet No: **1**

Location: **Green Lane Skate Park**

Date: **25 February 2009** Times: **9.30 a.m.–12 p.m.**

Cast required:	Lead male – Lewis Lead female – Paulina Extras in background – Lesley, Jo, Phil and Sarah
Crew required:	Camera – Mike Director – Natasha Props – Tom
Camera equipment:	Sony Handycam DCR-HC62E, tripod, mini DV tapes, charger and backup battery.
Lighting equipment:	None
Sound equipment:	Inbuilt in camera
Props:	Skateboard, kneepads, MP3 player, mobile phones, empty drinks cans and girls' bike.

Figure 7.1: Would you be able to fill in a call sheet like this one for one of your productions?

Continuity

You need to ensure that all of the footage that you have shot on any given day is of a good enough quality to take through to the editing stage. In order to do this, it is advisable to review all of your footage before you leave the location for the day. The reason for this is that you need to ensure **continuity** within your footage, so scenes that go together have the same backgrounds.

Continuity is something that is often overlooked in amateur productions and this can have a huge effect on the overall look of your productions. You should take account of and consider the time and effort required to ensure continuity and its overall effect on your final product.

Case study: Continuity

Here is a scenario that may result in continuity problems. You are filming outside in the daytime in the early spring; it is a sunny day, the clouds are being blown across the sky and the blossom is bursting on the trees.

You film your shots but when you get back to the editing suite and review your footage you realise that some of them are badly framed and unusable. This is only a few of the shots though, the majority were fine and exactly what you wanted. You are not scheduled to film again until two days later and the weather forecast is overcast and showery.

- What should you have done before leaving the original location shoot?
- What can be done to salvage the shots that are unusable?
- What will be the effect of filming the ruined footage on the next location shoot?

At the end of this process, you should have acquired a decent amount of footage that is now ready to be taken on to the post-production or editing phase, bringing you closer to your completed product. See Post-production, pages 174–180.

Audio production

You will encounter many different technologies throughout your course, some of which are specific to your chosen medium. In audio production, microphones are probably one of the most important; after all, they are what help you to capture the sounds you are trying to record! You should have already investigated different types of microphones and their uses in the investigation phase of your studies and, as a result, should be able to select your technology appropriately.

Similarly, the types of recording and editing formats (for example, digital, CD, hard disks or mixing desks) will depend on the technology available at your centre. Most recording nowadays is done digitally, as this allows for the best possible quality during capture and editing.

Table 7.1: Find out as much as you can about the equipment and formats available to you. Discuss with your classmates which option would be the best choice for your project.

Type of equipment	Option	Description
Format	Digital sound file, e.g. MP3, MP4	• Digital audio encoding format commonly used for storing audio. • Standard of digital audio compression for transfer and playback of music on digital audio players. • Compresses amount of data needed whilst producing a faithful reproduction of the original.
	CD	• Optical disc used to store digital data. • Compresses amount of data needed whilst producing a faithful reproduction of the original. Small physical size. • Initially used solely for audio, but can be used for other data storage as well. • Not indestructible so blemishes and stains can cause the CD to skip.
	Minidisc	• Digital recording and playback format. • Recordings can be erased and re-recorded over. Individual tracks may be deleted, or divided to allow editing on the minidisk recorder itself. • Much smaller than reel-to-reel audio tapes. • Imperfections on the playing size affect its performance.
	Digital audio tapes (DAT)	• Method of storing large amounts of audio in a compact format at a quality high enough for professional use. • Fragile and easily damaged. • Not instantly accessible; have to spool backwards and forwards to correct place.
Microphones (stereo/mono)	Omnidirectional	• Picks up sound that reaches it from any direction.
	Directional/ unidirectional	• Picks up sound that reaches it mainly from one direction.
	Rifle	• Highly directional; very good at picking up sounds from a particular direction. Often used in video where you do not want to see a hand holding a microphone on screen.
Recording device	Computer with editing software	• Recording directly into editing software in a studio, or using a laptop on location.
	Minidisc recorder	• Available in portable and studio versions.
	DAT recorder	• Available in portable and studio versions.

You will come into contact with most of the relevant technology during studio recording sessions, during which you will record your programme prior to editing. It is important for you to be familiar with studio layout and operation, as well as on-air and off-air protocols. You should also be able to monitor levels during the recording process. The activity below outlines a scenario for you and encourages you to work through the process in order to successfully record your footage.

Activity: Working in the studio

Here is an example of a typical studio layout, which may be similar to ones you will use in your own production work. Your school or college radio studio can be used for both live and recorded programming and can generally broadcast to a local area provided the necessary licences are obtained.

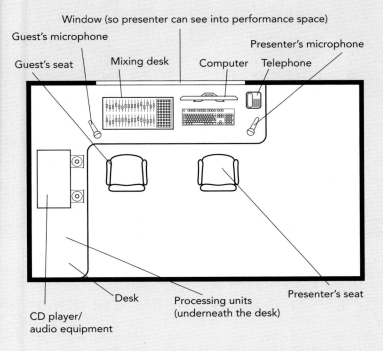

There are two ways of broadcasting a radio programme, one is using a pre-recorded programme and the other is using a live format. Both of these have advantages and disadvantages.

1. Can you list the disadvantages and advantages of both of these broadcast formats?

2. What can go wrong that may affect the quality and content?

3. Can you think of any instances where problems have occurred during a radio show you were listening to?

4. How were these problems dealt with by the DJ and technical staff?

Live recordings

When recording your footage, you will experience different working practices and how you will work will depend on the format. For example, you may be encouraged to undertake some live recordings, which will mean that you will be recording the programme at the same time it is being broadcast, much like *The Chris Moyles Show* on BBC Radio 1. These programmes can later be edited down and broadcast in formats such as podcasts so that listeners can catch up on what they missed.

Many radio shows are broadcast live. What are the advantages and disadvantages of working in this way?

As–live recordings

You can also pre-record footage that is scripted but would seem as though it were being broadcast live (see Figure 7.1 on page 156). These programmes will need to be lively and upbeat and still include links and jingles that bring the different sections together just as you would have in a live programme. As-live recording allows you to script and review what is being said, giving you more control over the process and ensuring that errors aren't made, such as overrun or people saying inappropriate things on air.

Interviews

Many radio programmes, whether factual or entertainment, will require the inclusion of interviews of some form or another. These can be done in two ways; they can either be:

• pre-recorded or put into a live broadcast

• recorded live but using previously scripted questions.

It is always best to research and script live interview questions for legal reasons, as you do not want to offend the interviewee or the listeners. Similar to interviews are commentaries and outside broadcasts; again, these need to be considered in terms of length and relevance and are probably best pre-recorded and inserted into a live programme to avoid sticky situations.

Activity: As-live recording session

You have produced a script for a music radio programme that is to be aired on the college radio during broadcast week. As it is impossible for the studio to be manned at all times because of lesson timetables, you need to produce an as-live recording to be played in the refectory during the day.

You are in the studio with your presenters and production crew and need to get your footage recorded within the hour. Given these time constraints, what can you do to ensure that the process runs smoothly?

What can you do to ensure that the programme has a 'live' feeling to it?

As you will be able to edit the tracks in to your programme later, focus on recording the presenters performing their links. The whole programme isn't going to contain just music so don't forget to include links to things such as traffic, weather and news updates.

Once you have finished recording your work, as with video production, be sure to review the footage to check that it is suitable. Although you will be able to do a lot to manipulate the final product during editing you can't add what you don't have and you can't always fade out or cut what you don't want!

Remember

As with video production, it is important to rehearse your script; however, this time it is you and not your actors who will have to rehearse. Practise your script regularly and keep in mind that, for a radio show, you are a presenter who needs to engage your audience: you need to be lively, upbeat and entertaining.

Production schedule

Week	Week beginning	Activity
1	7 April	Editing ident
2	14 April	Editing ident
3	21 April	Production file (research)
4	28 April	Production file (running order, script)
5	5 May	Transferring files on to the computer
6	12 May	Recording in the studio
7	19 May	Editing production
8	26 May	Editing production
9	2 June	Editing production
10	9 June	Evaluation

Figure 7.3: A production schedule. Try not to overcomplicate your schedule, but make sure it contains any information that will help you to keep on track. What other details do you think would be useful to add to this example?

Print production

Whatever technology is used, the process of printing remains broadly the same and involves the mass reproduction of words and images.

Different ways of printing

There are three main types of printing process:

- **Hand-operated** processes, including etching, linocut, woodcut and screen print

- **Mechanical** processes, including machinery such as offset, litho, flexography, gravure

- **Digital** processes, including laser printing, inkjet printing and desktop publishing (DTP) software

In print production work, there will be different technologies available to you but for the most part, unless your centre has highly-specialised equipment, you will be producing your products using current digital technology and software.

Although mechanical and digital print processes are used for nearly all commercial print products, many traditional hand-operated processes are still used for producing pieces of art, craft and design work.

Activity: Understanding printing processes

Look up the following printing processes. Write a short definition for each one, and try to find an example of a product that has been created using each process.

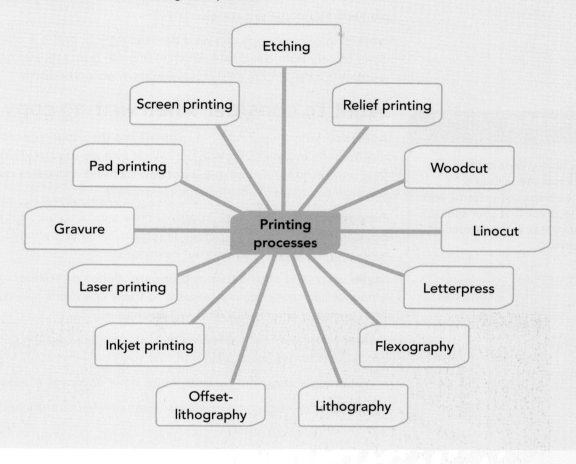

Different types of print product

There are many formats that your product can take, including:

- newspapers
- magazines
- posters
- leaflets
- booklets
- labels
- packaging.

Your chosen format will affect how you design and lay out your product, so you need to keep it in mind at all times during the production process. Changing the format once you have started the production process will affect not only your design and layout but also your written work.

Writing for print

The original writing that is used in a print product is called **copy**. When you are producing copy for your product, you will need to ensure that it is all your own work (and not copied from the Internet!) to avoid plagiarism or copyright issues.

Producing original copy can be a demanding job, and it is often done to very tight deadlines, which is why the print industry employs journalists, copywriters and professional writers and editors.

What to consider when writing copy

Audience: who is your target audience? Are they young or old? Are they experts or new to the subject? What else do they read? What are they interested in? Knowing the answers to these and other questions will help you to pitch your copy appropriately.

Purpose: are you writing to inform or entertain? Do you want people to buy something or are you persuading them to do something? Are you reporting the facts or giving your opinion?

Style: what style of writing is appropriate? Funny or serious? Hard-hitting or sympathetic? The answers to these questions may depend on the context or where your work will appear.

Genre: you should have decided on your genre during the pre-production stages. Here are some that you could consider:

- **reportage:** describing events; much news coverage is reportage

- **critique:** an evaluation or review, often used in entertainment coverage

- **editorial or commentary:** a personal viewpoint.

Ensuring the generic conventions of written work

When undertaking written and print production work, consider the genre that your work fits into, always keeping in mind the:

- format

- style

- layout

- audience.

You will have decided on an idea at the pre-production stage and you will now be working through that idea, bringing it to life and constructing the overall content. In order to do this, keep focused on

Remember

Accuracy is very important. Remember all the skills and techniques discussed in Unit 2 and be sure to check that your spelling, grammar, syntax and punctuation are all correct.

your genre and keep to hand some examples of similar products that you can reference to ensure that you are sticking to the right style.

- You can do this by looking at work of the same genre on the Internet and keeping a copy of the ones that are most relevant to your work.

- You can also (or may already) buy products such as newspapers and magazines that fit your genre. Physical products are often better to use as they give you a better idea of the overall look of the completed article you are hoping to create.

- Consider reviewing products from different genres as a means of contrast, which will help you keep in mind the things that you don't want to include, avoiding overlap and mixing of genres, which can confuse the audience.

When undertaking print work, you should also keep in mind the overall look and work closely to your original drafts and designs. This is not to say that you cannot change some of your ideas, but it is important not to be too radical and start changing the entire look and layout of a product at this stage. Doing this can do more harm than good and, rather than providing you with a new and improved product, you may end up with something that is incomplete, you may find yourself failing to meet your deadlines or you may find yourself with a finished product that fails to meet the requirements of the brief.

What do you need to consider when designing the layout for a printed media product?

The printing process

The choice of print technology is dependent on the type of product being printed, the quality of reproduction that is needed, the amount of money available and the size of the print run.

The printing process needs to be carefully monitored and controlled so that the same high quality can be maintained throughout the whole of the print run.

Case study: Yatin Valand, Printer

Yatin works as a printer in the Print Skills Centre of a college. After completing First Diploma and National Diploma qualifications he joined the Modern Apprenticeship scheme and started working in the centre's print department.

He was always more interested in the practical side of media production and operating the equipment – the job he has is one in which he can use his practical skills to the full.

He enjoys working in an area that uses the latest technology and can now take a design that has been developed on a computer, transfer it to a digital printer and see this work printed on to a variety of different forms and products, including leaflets, posters, T-shirts and mouse mats.

- What practical skills do you think that Yatin needs for his job?
- How can Yatin keep up to date with the latest technology?
- Other than those listed, can you think of any other formats that Yatin may be able to print designs on?

Digital media production

For your digital media production, you will be working with less paperwork but should have a good set of designs and plans from which to work. Whether you are creating a web page or computer game, the principles are the same and you will need to have thought carefully about your sound, text, video, graphics and animations. You may also have to consider areas such as 3-D content.

You may create your own content or you may decide to use content from other websites, in which case you will also have to consider the legal and ethical implications of importing **assets** from secondary sources and using them in your own work.

Your product will need to have sound interactive elements and good navigation capabilities or controls depending on the medium. Your graphics, layout and colour will need to be consistent, well thought out and user friendly.

Sourcing graphics and images

There are many different ways to source graphics and images; some can be original, of your own design and creation, others can be secondary materials from places like the Internet or software packages that you already have on your computer.

Where and how you source your images and graphics will depend on the medium and genre you are working in. If you are designing computer games or 2-D and 3-D images, the images and graphics will need to be your own, using your own original ideas and concepts. You can, however, use other sources for inspiration and possibly as guidance on the genre you are working in.

Some interactive media products, such as websites, will allow you more freedom of content. You will also be able to add links to other websites that are relevant to your own product, but you must always keep in mind infringement of copyright when using the intellectual property of others.

The digital media production process

A digital media product follows the same broad process as any other media product. The production stage includes the tasks involved in putting the product together. You may build a **prototype** in this stage, which is always a good idea if you are creating a high-value or innovative item.

The production process for digital media products is explained further in the following sections.

Producing the different parts

During the production stages, you will need to manage, build and test the different elements that make up your product. In the industry, these parts are often called 'deliverables'. The deliverables can be broken down into the following areas:

- Design and media deliverables include artwork, animations, audio, photos and/or video assets that will be included in your product.

- Content deliverables usually covers the bringing together of the copy (text) with design and media assets, and structuring them into the order that you want.

- Technology deliverables depend on the type of product that you are producing. They could be the webpages, DVDs or CDs.

Key term

Prototype – a working model that can be used to test the visual design, technical functionality and user experience.

The production cycle

Breaking the production process down into identifiable, manageable and trackable stages is particularly important for digital products. Thinking of it as a cycle will help you to focus on fixing problems early on, before it becomes too late or expensive to correct them. The production stages are outlined in Figure 7.4 below.

Prototype. Create a working model to test out with potential users. Try to test out the technical aspects, user experience and the visual design with a small amount of sample content.

Alpha build. The first full build. This should have as much of the content (including design and media assets) as possible. Think about whether you need audio in at this stage – it may be better to add it in when you know everything is working!

Beta build. This should include any fixes to bugs that you picked up in your alpha build. All the content and assets should be in at this stage. You should do extensive technical testing at this point.

Release candidate. A final chance to check everything is correct and working before creating the final product.

Gold Master. The finished product that you use for duplicating (in the case of DVDs and CDs) or uploading for release (for online products).

Figure 7.4: Flowchart showing the parts of the production process. Why do you think that it's important to create a prototype before the first full build?

Testing

Testing is an important part of the production process for digital products, and you should plan your testing carefully. You may want to test for different things at different stages, and you will need a test plan and test scripts to keep track of what you find and how you have fixed things. Here are just some of the things that you will need to test:

- **Content:** ideally you will have checked all your copy and media assets for accuracy and fitness for purpose before you started the production stages, but you should still check that everything appears as you want it to. For example, does video content display at the correct size, scale and quality?

- **Usability:** have you tested your prototype with users to check that they understand what to do with your product? Does the navigation work?

- **Functionality:** checking that buttons and/or links work, for example, does selecting 'Home', 'Menu', 'Next' or 'Back' take you to the correct place?

- **Accessibility:** can everyone access your product? Do you need to think about text-only versions of web pages, use of colour?

- **Technical testing:** there are two types of technical testing:

  - **Compatibility testing:** does a product work in, for example, the Windows® 7 operating system, Internet Explorer® 8 web browser and MAC OSX operating system software, and on the iPhone mobile digital device?

  - **Performance testing:** does a CD product run quickly enough? Is a website product set up to run at the best speed? Can it cope with a large number of visitors to the site?

Case study: Andy Shaw, User Interface Designer and Project Manager

I work for Sandbox Media Ltd, a small Bristol-based digital design agency with a reputation rooted firmly on delivering creative, intelligent websites, interactive media and online marketing solutions for public and private sector clients. Using 'agile' processes, we focus on transparent project management, **progressive web standards** and rich user experiences.

One specific area we work in is the design and development of CMS (Content Management System) websites. This type of site offers the client far more control than static websites, enabling them to keep content up-to-date, without the need to contact their web developers every time something needs changing.

Generally speaking, we break projects down into four key stages:

Stage 1 – Strategy and planning

This stage concentrates on analysis and consideration of project requirements. Following an initial deconstruction of the 'big picture' we focus on planning the structure of the project, from the ground up.

During this stage, we will start creating **wireframes**, user stories, prototypes, content audits, moodboards and sitemaps.

Stage 2 – User interface design

Taking direct influence from the artefacts developed in Stage 1 we then shift our attention to the 'aesthetic', i.e. developing the 'look and feel' of the site. Following design sign-off we then move on to Stage 3.

Stage 3 – Development and testing

The 'test' site is set up on our version-controlled development server; installing the chosen CMS framework and creating any bespoke elements. The design is then applied to the framework and the functionality of the system is verified against acceptance tests.

Stage 4 – Documentation and sign-off

The final stage concentrates on the migration of the site from development server to live server, which means the site is now 'live' and available for viewing on the web.

- What personal attributes and skills do you think that Andy needs for his job?
- Can you find any examples of CMS websites?
- Why do you think that it's important to set up a test site on a development server rather than on the live server?

Key terms

Progressive web standards – using the most up-to-date usability and accessibility standards and guidelines available at the time of production.

Wireframes – detailed sketches showing the types of content and on-screen position of assets. These can be created in presentation or drawing software programs.

Assessment activity 7.1

When addressing these learning outcomes, you will be required to undertake production work in your chosen area. It is very likely that you will work as part of a production team, but you will be required to produce your own production work.

The work for this learning outcome will often be assessed by your tutor through:

- observations of your working practices
- submission of relevant documentation, production logs and diaries
- the final product.

Your aim is to create a finished product that realises its intentions, by following appropriate conventions and taking on an appropriate technical role.

Grading tips

To aim for a **merit**, you will need to produce a finished product that shows a sound level of competence in all areas, such as understanding and applying appropriate conventions, displaying sound technical skills and realising the intention either set out in the brief or decided on during pre-production.

To aim for a **distinction**, you will need to produce a finished product that shows a good level of competence in all areas, such as understanding and applying appropriate conventions, displaying fluent technical skills and clearly realising the intention either set out in the brief or decided on during pre-production.

PLTS

Organising your time and resources, and prioritising actions when producing a media product, whether working on your own or in a group, will help you to develop your skills as a **self-manager**.

Functional skills

Creating a project portfolio, ideas, notes and production documentation, and writing treatments, scripts, schedules, testing reports and reflective comments, will help you to develop your **English** skills.

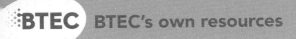

Learning outcomes

Unit	Name	Learning outcome
5	Video production	LO2 be able to contribute in a technical capacity to the creation of a video product
6	Audio production	LO2 be able to use audio technology to create an audio product
7	Print production	LO3 be able to create print products
8	Interactive media production	LO3 be able to create an interactive media product
9	Photography techniques	LO2 be able to use photographic technology to create photographic images
10	Animation techniques	LO3 be able to create an animation sequence
11	Web authoring	LO3 be able to use web authoring software to create a website
16	2D computer game engines	LO4 be able to build a 2D game world to a specification
17	3D computer game engines	LO4 be able to build a 3D game world to a specification
18	Advertising production	LO3 be able to create an advertisement
19	Writing for the creative media	LO3 be able to produce written material
20	Factual production for the creative media	LO3 be able to create a factual media product following appropriate conventions
21	Creative media production project	LO3 be able to create a proposed media product

WorkSpace Isabella Harris
Camera operator

My job as a camera operator has offered me a lot of variety and many challenges over the years. The production process can be very unpredictable at times, as there are so many people all working together to get the footage you need. Live recordings are especially challenging as they can be quite hectic and full on!

Working on my first live studio programme, which was a season finale of *Stars in Their Eyes*, was an exciting experience. It was a lot more elaborate than the pre-recorded versions we were used to, with a live orchestra and the pressure of filming the shots straight to a television audience of millions. The rehearsals, concentration and teamwork skills were extensive, but worth it when the programme was successfully aired.

It is important to follow all of the production paperwork to the letter and to be fully familiar with the content of the script and storyboard. In camerawork, the storyboard is what we work from for the most part, as well as taking on the vision of the director. Pre-recorded stuff is a lot easier to do, as you are able to cover up errors by re-shooting scenes; however, you can't just keep doing things over, at the end of the day, you have a schedule to work to and if you overrun that costs the company money.

In many respects, my job is pretty intense and my working day is packed with physical and mental activities; it can be really tiring. That said, when you eventually see the results of your labours, a final, fully-edited programme, aired on national television, it really is all worthwhile.

Think about it

1. How important is production paperwork to the production process?
2. What is the difference between pre-recorded and live production?
3. What are the potential problems that can occur during live production work?
4. What are the skills required to take part in live production work?

Just checking

1. What production paperwork is required for video production?
2. What paperwork is required for audio production?
3. What paperwork is required for print or photographic production?
4. Why is it important to keep detailed records of production processes?
5. What is a risk assessment and why is it necessary?
6. What are some of the potential hazards that you may have to deal with on a production?
7. What does the term 'continuity' mean? Where in your production work is it relevant?
8. What are some of the key points to remember during written production work?
9. What is the difference between graphics and images?
10. Why is it important to keep in mind copyright when sourcing images from the Internet?

Assignment tips

- Always ensure that you use relevant and detailed documentation when carrying out risk assessments for production activities and provide all group members with copies beforehand.
- When recording footage for video or audio production, make sure you log and label it all. This will keep it in order and help you to find it easily later.
- When working on location, always review recorded footage to make sure you have what you need. Remember that location conditions can change daily and there is no guarantee you will be able to match later footage and ensure continuity.
- Always print draft copies of your written and print work so you can review it before committing to a final copy.
- Check your sources and content when producing interactive media to ensure you don't infringe copyright.
- Most importantly, be methodical: check and refer to your paperwork regularly to make sure you keep on track. Don't rush things or you could end up making costly mistakes.

Post-production

This section deals with the work you will do after you have captured or created the necessary content for your media product. You will look at how to finalise and polish off your end product to a high standard, and what processes and paperwork you will need to use in order to do this.

In the film and television industries, post-production takes the form of editing footage on computers using digital software. Similarly, audio products can also be edited in this way and digitally altered or enhanced to suit the needs and purpose of the production. In photography and digital imaging, the post-production phase is about image manipulation in order to make the final product suit the required outcome.

The post-production stage is the final point at which changes, embellishments and improvements can be made to your product. With that in mind, it is important that you use appropriate software packages effectively to ensure that your product is sound and fit for purpose. Lack of care and consideration during the editing process can result in a final product that lacks cohesion, style and continuity.

Learning outcomes

The table on page 188 shows some of the optional units that contain a learning outcome requiring you to take part in a particular post-production activity. This is usually LO3 in any particular unit, but can also be LO2 as this element is targeted through your production work.

171

Assessment and grading criteria

Each optional unit shows you what you need to do in order to achieve a **pass**, **merit** or **distinction** grade for the post-production related learning outcome. These are all broadly the same and involve you producing a folder of evidence to show the processes that you went through during the post-production stage.

The table below shows you the relevant grading criteria for a sample of the optional units.

5 Video production

P3 apply video post-production techniques to the creation of a video product	**M3** demonstrate competent application of video post-production techniques to the creation of a video product	**D3** demonstrate skilful application of video post-production techniques to the creation of a video product

6 Audio production

P2 use audio technology to create an audio product that partially realises intentions	**M2** use audio technology competently to create an audio product that mainly realises intentions	**D2** use audio technology skilfully to create an audio product that clearly realises intentions

9 Photography techniques

P2 use photographic technology to create photographs that partially realise intentions	**M2** use photographic technology competently to create photographs that mainly realise intentions	**D2** use photographic technology skilfully to create photographs which clearly achieve intentions

10 Animation techniques

P3 use animation techniques to create an animation sequence that partially realises intentions	**M3** use animation techniques competently to create an animation sequence that mainly realises intentions	**D3** use animation techniques skilfully to create an animation sequence that clearly realises intentions

18 Advertising production

P3 use appropriate techniques and technology to create an advertisement that partially realises intentions	**M3** use appropriate techniques and technology competently to create an advertisement that mainly realises intentions	**D3** use appropriate techniques and technology skilfully to create an advertisement that clearly realises intentions

20 Factual production for the creative media

P3 apply appropriate conventions and use appropriate technology to create a factual media product that partially realises intentions	**M3** apply appropriate conventions and use appropriate technology competently to create a factual media product that mainly realises intentions	**D3** apply appropriate conventions and use appropriate technology skilfully to create a factual media product that clearly realises intentions

How you will be assessed

Assessment for the post-production element of each of the optional units will take the form of a completed product in an appropriate format. Work required for these learning outcomes will be undertaken as part of your production work, such as video or audio production, and your tutor is likely to track your progress through an integrated assignment, rather than by separate assessment. Work submitted may be subject to sampling by your centre's External Verifier as part of Edexcel's ongoing quality assurance procedures.

Your assessment could be in the form of:

- completed post-production paperwork
- a written explanation of post-production roles and work undertaken
- a completed product
- tutor observation of working practices and contributions.

Danielle, Audio production

Post-production has been my favourite part of production work over the last year. In my audio production unit, it was the time I got to mix things up a bit and mess around with ideas and sounds.

After I had finished recording my vocals, I would spend hours adding music and mixing links to create a music programme for broadcast on our college radio. We had to get pre-recorded material together for this because we couldn't always have someone manning the studio and we wanted to make the most of our broadcasting slots.

I found it easy to use the software, and this meant I could enjoy what I was doing. The software enabled me to cut and move about sections of my work, so I could overlap or separate speech or other sounds to make my programme smoother and sound better.

Although I do really enjoy doing live programmes and broadcasts, I have to say that I am happiest when I can sit with pre-recorded footage and change it to suit my needs. Working this way gives me much more control over the production: I can write the scripts and tell people what to say and then use the running order to knock it all together on the computer; it also means I get to choose my favourite sounds to add!

- What does digital editing software allow you to do with recorded footage?
- What do you think the difference is between the post-production for a live piece and a recorded piece?
- Is there any post-production paperwork mentioned? If so, what is it and why is it relevant?

Audio-visual post-production

There are many skills required for audio-visual post-production; this is because you are dealing with a medium that requires you to edit together images and sound. In the television and film industries, editing is a highly-skilled job as it is here that all of the special effects are added and continuity is checked.

Most editing today is **digital** and the old **analogue** tape machines that took video formats will one day become a thing of the past. The digital editing system allows footage to be cut up and moved about at the click of a mouse, whereas the analogue system involves footage being transferred from tape to tape using a near manual system. **Linear editing** skills are being used less and less in most areas of the industry and, as a result, are less likely to be taught in schools and colleges. It is more likely that you will experience a form of editing that is much closer to what is used in the industry today, where editing is carried out digitally using a variety of different software packages.

Key terms

Digital – the editing system currently used in the industry.

Analogue – an older and soon to be outdated system of broadcast and data transfer.

Linear editing

Linear editing, as the name suggests, is a more straightforward, one-way type of editing. In this process, a tape containing footage will be placed into a machine similar to the one pictured below.

The images from the tape are then played through a professional monitor and the required footage is recorded on to another tape in a different machine; this form of editing is also known as **tape-to-tape editing**.

What are the advantages and disadvantages of linear editing?

The machine containing the tape with the footage can be played and then rewound manually so it can be reviewed frame by frame using a special control that slows down playback. Each piece of footage will then be captured on to the blank tape in final order before the audio is synced back in.

Although these techniques and technologies are not often used today, they can still be helpful when editing news reports that have been filmed on location. This is because linear editing provides a quicker way of editing footage without having to upload it first.

Non-linear editing

This is the type of editing you are more used to and that you will probably use in your school or college. It is strongly favoured in the film and animation industries and allows for visuals and audio to be split or added according to need. There is also the possibility of adding much better visuals, such as transitions and special effects, as well as cleaner and sharper sound and images.

Today, most film footage and audio recordings have been digitally edited using equipment similar to that pictured below.

Which non-linear editing techniques are you most likely to use while working on your own products?

Think about it

Video editing technology has changed and developed dramatically over the years. Try to create a timeline that identifies key breakthroughs in technology.

There are many different editing software packages available today for all types of computers. You can edit at home, school or work on PCs, laptops, notebooks and Mac computers. You can even edit images on your mobile phone!

Some relatively basic packages that you may come into contact with, such as Windows Movie Maker or the iMovie application program, are provided free with other software, while others are more advanced and have to be paid for, such as Adobe® Premiere® Pro and Adobe Audition.

The packages used in the industry are more advanced, especially when it comes to areas such as adding digital effects and computer animations. It is important to realise the extent and limitations of the packages you are likely to use and you may find it helpful to conduct some research into editing equipment and technology.

Activity: Digital editing software

1. Look into the software package available at your school or college and make a note of its capabilities in terms of effects, transitions and so on.

2. Now investigate a package that you consider to be the next step up from the one you are using and compare the capabilities of this to yours.

3. Finally, find information on more professional software packages such as those used by Disney Pixar. These are likely to be professionally made and programmed and will not be available for general sale but will have some amazing capabilities.

Once you have done these comparisons, you will have a better insight into the editing process and the many different types of software available to help you create that all important on screen magic!

Did you know?

Almost every frame of *The Lord of The Rings* trilogy has some form of special effect in it, whether it be shrinking actors to the size of hobbits or adding fictional characters such as Gollum or the orcs, even creating such magnificent structures as the Two Towers or the Elven land of Rivendell.

It is estimated that the total cost of each movie was in the region of $100 million as a result of all of the special effects required to make everything seem so realistic. All of these effects were computer generated and would have been added during post-production.

Processes and paperwork

Once the footage has been captured, it is necessary to review and then capture it on to your chosen software package. There are processes that you will need to go through in order to do this and paperwork that you will need to fill in so that you can keep track of what footage is where, ready for you to find again later.

Below is an example of a document that you may use in order to log your footage. Such documentation requires you to make a note of the time code (this can be found on the camera or computer screen), which reflects where in the tape your chosen footage is. You should also keep a reference of which tape you are sourcing that footage from, so make sure all tapes are labelled correctly. Providing details of the group the tape belongs to will give you an idea of who the editing is being done for. Further information about who is doing the editing and when is also beneficial.

Edit decision list

Time code	Outline of shot	Keep/discard	Duration (secs)
10.36.32	Teacher enters room	Keep	35.00
11.55.20	CU of television screen	Discard	1.26
12.05.13	CU of computer screen	Keep	2.55
14.22.05	MS gang running from shop	Keep	11.09
17.01.30	LS sunset over hills	Discard	9.44

Figure 8.1: An example of an edit decision list, used for video or film footage. Use this sample to help you complete your own.

When going through your footage, record all relevant information on your documentation. For example, by noting how long your shots should last you can get an overall idea of how long your final piece is going to be. Similarly, if you have been provided with a brief that requires you to produce a product of a certain length then you can use this to ensure that you don't overrun and that all footage is used advantageously.

Activity: Filling in paperwork for video post-production

This activity will help you to practise using post-production paperwork and get you into the habit of reviewing footage correctly. Use the template provided below when reviewing your production work and refer back to the completed sample on page 177 to help you work out what information you need to fill in.

Group name:		Tape no:	
Editor:		Date:	

Time code	Outline of shot	Keep/ discard	Duration (secs)

Once you have viewed and logged your footage, you need to go through the process of capturing and editing it into the required order. Use your paperwork to ensure that you only capture what you need.

The following two sections outline the process by which video footage is captured and edited on non-linear digital software packages.

Using a FireWire serial bus

There is a port in your camera and a corresponding one on your computer that will take a FireWire lead and it is this that you use to capture your footage on to the computer. The image below shows the plugs on a FireWire lead. They go in the corresponding shaped sockets on the camera and computer, but remember that these can vary depending on make and model.

Try to identify the FireWire sockets on the cameras and computers you will be using for your own media production.

Footage capture

Once your software package is opened and your FireWire is connected to the camera and the computer, you need to select the necessary function from your package in order to capture your footage.

This may sound simplistic, but there are different systems for different packages and there is a process that needs to be followed in order to capture and store footage.

1. First you need to select the option that allows you to capture footage from a digital camera and then follow the instructions provided on the screen. Always choose the best quality for your device or the default option for footage quality.

Key terms

Trimming – the process by which you cut down your chosen clips.

Timeline – the view of your product that will be provided at the bottom of the screen when using footage capture software during audio-visual post-production.

Titles – during audio-visual post-production, these can be added anywhere within your footage but are always required at the start and finish.

Transitions (audio-visual post-production) – also known as cuts, fades, wipes and so on; allow for a smoother 'transition' between clips.

Rendering – rendering should not be done until the end of the editing process; this is because rendered footage cannot be altered.

2. You will probably be prompted to decide whether to capture the whole footage from the tape or to capture the footage manually. As you have gone to the time and effort to fill out all of your paperwork, the manual option is the best choice here and also allows you better editorial control.

3. Once you have done this, the footage will start playing from your camera and you will need to begin marking in and out points. This means that you will have to select **Start capture** and **Stop capture** (or their equivalents) at the correct points in your footage.

4. When all of the required footage has been selected and captured, save your clips to your project so you can begin placing them on your timeline.

All clips will need to be dragged across to the preview box and reviewed before they are placed on the timeline. This process is different with each software package, as is the place in which 'trimming' of your clips will take place. The following key terms will help you with this process.

- **Trimming** – the process by which you cut down your chosen clips to ensure that there are no loose edges or overlap with other clips allowing for smoother transitions.

- **Timeline** – the view of your product that will be provided at the bottom of the screen when using footage capture software during audio-visual post-production. The timeline can be added to as you build your footage clip by clip. As the name suggests, it provides a chronological view of your product from start to finish. Pressing the space bar will often allow you to view the footage you have built up in the preview box.

- **Titles** – during audio-visual post-production, these can be added anywhere within your footage but are always required at the start and finish so that you can add the title of your product and credits at the end.

- **Transitions** (audio-visual post-production) – also known as **cuts**, **fades**, **wipes** and so on. These allow for a smoother 'transition' between clips and some packages offer effects such as images bouncing in and out or up and down. They should be selected with care and be relevant to your chosen product.

- **Rendering** – the need to render footage is dependent on the software package being used for audio-visual post-production. It should not be done until the end of the editing process, when all footage is in the desired order and you are certain that no more changes need to be made; this is because rendered footage cannot be altered.

Audio post-production

The need for post-production in an audio production, such as a radio programme, is entirely dependent on your producing a pre-recorded or 'as-live' product, as it is not required during live programme production. As with video production, the editing process will take place after you have recorded the required footage so that you can tidy up the dialogue and add **links** and sound effects.

Editing packages will also differ according to availability, but, for the most part, the processes will be similar and have the same outcome.

Processes and paperwork

Once you have recorded your footage, the document you are likely to find the most helpful is your **running order**, as this outlines what the content of the show should be. You can then use this document to help put your footage into the correct order, making sure that you have remembered to add your links and any sound effects required.

The following activity contains a sample of a running order that you can use during post-production.

Activity: Filling in paperwork for audio post-production

As with the video post-production section, it is important for you to get used to filling in paperwork prior to undertaking any editing work.

The running order contains details of the content of the radio programme, usually indicated by the start of the dialogue shown in the link boxes or by the name of the song or sound effect. There are also details of the length of the link and the time code that relates to the required footage.

Try to create your own running order for a pre-recorded show. An entertainment programme such as a 'breakfast' or 'drive time' show are good options for this task, as they are lively and fast paced so will contain a lot of links between the DJ and music.

ITEM NO.	ITEM	DURATION	START	FINISH
1	Station Stab	00.30	00.00	00.30
2	Elbow *Grounds for Divorce*	04.00	00.30	04.30
3	Link 1 (on today's show)	00.30	04.30	05.00
4	M.I.A. *Paper Planes*	03.30	05.00	08.30
5	Station Stab	00.30	08.30	09.00
6	Klaxons *Golden Skans*	04.00	09.00	13.00
7	Link 2 (You're listening to)	00.30	13.00	13.30
8	Kanye West *Homecoming*	04.00	13.30	17.30

Editing software

It is likely that your centre will use software packages such as Adobe Audition. This is a good starting point for audio editing and allows you the flexibility to cut and move footage using a digital format, which is clearer than analogue and will provide a better quality final product.

Adobe Audition allows you to lay down tracks in a linear order and insert speech sections to 'link' the tracks together. This turns the random pieces of footage into a more recognisable format, much like the radio shows you hear on local and national radio. The only real difference between this work and that done in a professional studio is that many stations will broadcast live and be manned throughout the night.

Footage transfer and manipulation

Once you have filled in all of the necessary paperwork and recorded all of your footage, it will be necessary to transfer it to your chosen editing software and put it in the correct order. Much like video post-production, this process will require data transfer and the manipulation of footage into a correct order on a timeline.

Check that you have all of the footage you need and that you have space to work with. This means that you will be able to shorten your footage to cut out any overrun in timing or mistakes made by the DJ, without causing the final product to seem jumpy or out of sync. It is good practice to record a few versions of your work – maybe two or three – during the production stage, so you can pick the best bit to work with in post-production.

Links and idents

Modern radio stations, although often permanently manned and broadcasting live, will have a stockpile of clips such as links and **idents** (programme or station identification) that will be pre-recorded and added into the programme by the DJ during broadcast. These can take many forms and have many different purposes, for example:

- some may be used to add comedy effect
- some may be used as a backing track whilst the DJ speaks, introducing the next track
- some may be used to introduce different segments of the show, for example, news, sports and travel sections.

Whatever the purpose, these soundtracks will need to be recorded in a studio and reviewed before they are used on the programme. Some will have fades and transitions added to them, voiceovers may have music added to liven them up and some will have the levels and pitch adjusted so that they are clearer and easy to listen to.

Activity: Recording links and idents

The recording of these clips is often done separately to the main body of the programme. This means you will use your DJ, voiceover artists and possibly musicians to record the footage needed to make up the link or jingle.

Make sure you have a clear idea of how you want the programme to run and where you want your links or jingles to be so that you can place them into the main body of your programme.

Take your vocals and mix them with your music beds so that they work together well and are catchy; after all, you want your audience to remember them.

Try playing around with the sound levels and fading in and out so the transition between sections is seamless.

Finally, place the links and idents on your timeline and playback the footage to assess how well they fit with the rest of the programme content.

Many schools and colleges use pre-recording and editing processes to produce radio programmes. This is because it is unlikely that every centre has the facilities to undertake live broadcasts. The skills that you will learn are essential to a future career in audio production, as pre-recording footage is common practice within the industry.

Case study: Ken Sato, Audio production lecturer

The learners on my course work hard in the studio recording their footage, so it is important to ensure that they get things right in the classroom editing their material together.

When they open their files from their N-drive, they need to place the footage on to a sequencing multi-track, which allows them to cut it down to get rid of any mistakes. Usually, when they are in the studio, there is a time delay between pressing the record button and when they start to speak, so there is space either side to trim the footage if necessary.

At the college, we have a good selection of tracks for the learners to choose from. They can use these to help create their links and idents, and sequence them as they go along.

When they have finished their work, they save it and send it to me. During broadcast weeks, I use the pre-recorded programmes to add to the playlist and they are broadcast overnight when the station is unmanned. I generally need eight one-hour shows to fit the required time slots, which means that during a broadcast week everyone gets to show off their DJ talents as well as their production skills!

- What is the first thing learners need to do before they begin editing?

- Why is it useful to have some extra space before and after each piece of recorded footage?

- What happens to the pre-recorded programmes that learners have edited?

Photography techniques

This unit is similar to audio and video production, as it requires you to capture original footage and then transfer it to either a software package or darkroom where the images can be manipulated and altered to suit the overall intentions of the product. Today it is more likely that you will use digital image capture and manipulation, much like the processes used in the industry; however, there is still a need for understanding of the more 'traditional' techniques that you would use in a darkroom.

This section looks at the process of image manipulation in both of these areas and provides you with guidance as to how these processes can aid your overall product. Look through a magazine or newspaper and find an advertisement that uses a celebrity to promote a product. Do you think this image is truly representative of how this person looks in real life? What do you think has been done to the image to make it more appealing to its intended audience?

Did you know?

A large percentage of the photographic images we see in the media have been enhanced, altered or manipulated in some way, in order to create the desired image or effect. Even factual products such as newspapers can contain manipulated images, whether it is the main content or the background that has been altered. However, newspapers have to be a little more careful about how they represent images as they are subject to strict codes of conduct regulating representation of content.

Image manipulation

Image manipulation allows you to represent your final product in a manner that suits your purpose or medium. Traditionally, image manipulation would take place in a darkroom and the photographer would use different solutions or mixes of solutions to create an overall effect. Manipulation could be as simple as choosing to blur an image by under developing it or by scratching the print to make it seem messy and rough around the edges. Traditional methods can also include the use of airbrushing in order to retouch images and make them seem faultless.

Newer digital image manipulation is much more advanced. Some of it can take place on the camera, such as cropping or rotating an image, and you can even do this on your mobile phone.

Using modern technology to change the look or even the content of a photo is also possible and doing so can change the meaning of the image. Backgrounds and people can be removed from images; similarly, things can be added and blended in to make them look as if they were there in the first place. It can be argued that with modern photography techniques, similar to modern editing techniques, it is hard to trust that what you see is real!

In terms of your own production work, you are more likely to use digital cameras and photo editing software, such as Adobe® Photoshop® software, to produce your images. It is important to exercise some editorial control over what you do and how you present your images to the audience. Always keep in mind the point you are trying to make and what you are trying to represent.

The following photos highlight how image manipulation can be used to alter an image to make it more pleasing to look at. In addition, the whole meaning or concept of a photograph can be changed by adding or removing objects, people, light, shadows and so on.

What differences can you see between these two images?

Case study: Ivan Korskii, Professional photographer

I have been working as a professional photographer for the past five years and have my own studio, which I use to do family photography and professional photo shoots. I also do wedding photography. I would say that the majority of the work I do is digitally manipulated or 'enhanced'.

The work I do with families is less likely to be touched up than the wedding photos or promotional and publicity shots. If I do glamour shots, I always alter the image slightly to give it a softer, more romantic, hazy feel and I will remove any blemishes that might be obvious and ruin the overall look.

Wedding photos often need a bit of work to be done on them because a wedding is a really big event in people's lives, hopefully never to be repeated.

The bride always wants a picture in which she looks glowing and glamorous and that is what I provide.

Obviously, publicity shots are worked on the most because people are trying to promote themselves to the outside world and want to be seen in the best light possible. However, you can't change the person's features as this would misrepresent them to others and, in my opinion, that is not what image manipulation is about.

- When is Ivan most likely to 'touch up' shots?
- Why does he do this and what effect does it have on the finished product?
- What does Ivan say he can't change in a photo? Why not?

Finishing and placement or mounting

This stage of the process involves presenting your work so that it has the right effect on the intended audience. If you have taken your picture for the purpose of adding it to another media product then you will need to consider its placement within the overall layout so that it has the most impact.

If you are working on a magazine or non-factual product, you will want your picture to be appealing and eye catching and to provide content to the accompanying article. For example, a fashion page will require pictures of models looking good in the clothes you are reviewing. A band review will need some performance images to show how they look on stage to attract the target audience.

If your picture is intended to be placed in a factual product, such as a newspaper or real-life story, then it will need to illustrate the point being made and be slightly more hard hitting. This means that placement may need to be more central.

For example, a newspaper article describing the deaths of soldiers in Afghanistan may use photographs of the deceased alongside a more hard-hitting image of the combat zone (perhaps showing someone wounded) to provoke an emotional response in the reader.

The type of genre you are working in will influence all your decisions regarding how you finish or mount your picture to gain the maximum effect possible.

Relating these techniques to other production units

The techniques discussed in this chapter are mostly found in photographic audio and video production, but can also be used to create products in other units. Interactive media production, such as video games and websites, involve an ongoing production process, as does print production. This is because the final product is built up as you go along and there is no 'finishing' required.

The units outlined below may require you to produce an audio-visual, audio or photographic product and, as such, will require you to undertake post-production techniques.

Advertising production

If you reflect on everyday life, you will realise that there is advertising everywhere and that it is shown on all mediums, including:

- television
- film
- radio
- print
- the Internet.

You will need to keep your audience and product in mind at all times, but in some cases you will be required to use the post-production techniques outlined in this chapter to ensure your product is completed to the best possible standard.

Factual production for the creative media

Although factual production can cover many areas from print to interactive media, there is the possibility that you will choose to create a factual product that involves audio-visual and audio formats, as well as visual formats. You may choose to make a documentary that deals with facts and figures or produce photographs that add emphasis to a news or magazine article; whichever option you choose, you will need to follow the guidelines outlined in this chapter and keep in mind the professional practices of your chosen medium.

> **Think about it**
>
> How many types of media product can you think of that have to go through a post-production phase prior to distribution?

PLTS

Working towards goals, and showing initiative, commitment and perseverance whilst compiling footage in the post-production phase, will help you to develop your skills as a **self-manager**.

Functional skills

Capturing footage into appropriate file names and folders, keeping a record of file contents in a spreadsheet or table and editing footage, will help you to develop your **ICT** skills.

BTEC Assessment activity 8.1

When addressing these learning outcomes, you will be required to undertake post-production work in your chosen area. It is very likely that you will work as part of a production team, but you will be required to carry out your own post-production work to some extent.

The work for this learning outcome will often be assessed by your tutor through:

- observations of your working practices
- submission of relevant documentation, production logs and diaries
- the final product.

You should apply post-production techniques to your work so that the product you produce matches your original ideas and concepts.

Grading tips

To aim for a **merit**, you will need to ensure that you use post-production paperwork, techniques and technology to a good level to show competence in your abilities and to produce a final product that realises your original ideas and concepts.

To aim for a **distinction**, you will need to ensure that you use post-production paperwork, techniques and technology to a high standard to show all-round competence in your abilities and to produce a final product that fully realises and matches your original ideas and concepts.

Learning outcomes

Unit	Name	Learning outcome
5	Video production	LO3 be able to carry out post-production for a video product
6	Audio production	LO2 be able to use audio technology to create an audio product
9	Photography techniques	LO2 be able to use photographic technology to create photographic images
10	Animation techniques	LO3 be able to create an animation sequence
18	Advertising production	LO3 be able to create an advertisement
20	Factual production for the creative media	LO3 be able to create a factual media product following appropriate conventions

I have always been interested in the fine detail in life and I like to make sure that everything is in order, so it was hardly surprising when I became interested in post-production at college.

I love programme and film making and wanted to look for a career that suited my interests and allowed me to work on different projects. I began working for a small production company that made programmes for businesses and soon realised that my talents were better suited to the editing suite than behind the camera.

Although I was good at camera work, I found that I didn't enjoy waiting around for scenes to be set up and I hated repeating takes to get the right shots. I much preferred it if the footage was all recorded and handed over to me so that I could make some sense of it. I get a lot of enjoyment from making different clips fit together on a timeline and adding effects and transitions to bring them to life. I find working with soundtracks the most challenging, as it can be hard to sync clips together and make sure an actor's mouth is moving in time with the audio!

I soon decided to set up my own business so I could choose the type of work that I wanted to do and hire people to do the stuff I didn't enjoy as much. I have now worked on many different products for different companies, making adverts, promotional videos and training programmes. The work I do is often solitary but can also involve working closely with a director. It requires high levels of concentration, precision and attention to detail to ensure continuity.

My skills come in handy at home too, as I probably have one of the most precisely edited collections of family movies, and my kids are already having a go at putting footage together in my editing suite.

Think about it

1. What does the editing process entail?
2. What can happen to audio and visual footage during editing?
3. What are the main qualities Warwick states as being essential to ensure continuity?

Just checking

1. What paperwork will you need to use during video post-production?
2. List the stages of footage transfer in video editing.
3. What is a timeline and how do you use it?
4. What are transitions?
5. Can you name some relevant video-editing software packages and explain what they allow you to do?
6. What paperwork will you need to use during audio post-production?
7. What are links and idents?
8. Can you name some relevant audio-editing software packages and explain what they allow you to do?
9. Why are photographic images manipulated?
10. How can you manipulate photographic images?
11. Can you name some relevant photographic-editing software packages and explain what they allow you to do?

Assignment tips

- Keep your paperwork in good order and make sure it is all filled in neatly and correctly. These are working documents and you will need to refer to them at all times. Remember, if you can't read it, you can't use it!
- Patience is a virtue during the editing process. Try to stay calm and focused at all times and take regular breaks from your work to keep yourself fresh.
- Review your product regularly throughout the post-production process to ensure that it is turning out the way you want it.
- Be sure to save and store your work correctly so that it can be retrieved easily and worked on again.
- Before copying your final product on to a relevant format, ask someone else to look over it and give you some feedback. A pair of fresh eyes can often spot minor mistakes you might have overlooked.

Review

The ability to review and evaluate your product and production processes can provide you with invaluable information that could inform the choices you make for future ideas and products. In the creative media sector, reflective and evaluative work is essential to ensure that the correct products and services are reaching the correct or target audience.

Film, television and radio companies will use consumer feedback, as well as analysis of viewing and listening figures, to allow them to understand what is popular with any given audience at any particular time. Newspapers will monitor distribution figures and invite consumer feedback to ensure they have the right content and availability for their readers. Even the government will hold focus groups to find out what people think about their plans and policies or to measure the response of the voters to what they have done in the past.

Learning outcomes

The table on page 208 shows some of the optional units that contain a learning outcome requiring you to take part in a particular evaluation activity. This is usually LO4 in any particular unit, but can sometimes also be LO3.

Assessment and grading criteria

Each optional unit shows you what you need to do in order to achieve a **pass**, **merit** or **distinction** grade for the review related learning outcome. These are all broadly the same and involve you producing a folder of evidence to show the processes that you went through during the review stage.

The table below shows you the relevant grading criteria for a sample of the optional units. Further optional units with a review element are shown on page 218.

5 Video production

P4 review strengths and weaknesses of own video production work	**M4** describe strengths and weaknesses of own video production work with some detail and with reference to appropriate illustrative examples	**D4** evaluate strengths and weaknesses of own video production work with reference to precise and detailed illustrative examples

6 Audio production

P3 review strengths and weaknesses of own audio production work	**M3** describe strengths and weaknesses of own audio production work with some detail and with reference to appropriate illustrative examples	**D3** evaluate strengths and weaknesses of own audio production work with reference to precise and detailed illustrative examples

7 Print production

P4 review strengths and weaknesses of own print production work	**M4** describe strengths and weaknesses of own print production work with some detail and with reference to appropriate illustrative examples	**D4** evaluate strengths and weaknesses of own print production work with reference to precise and detailed illustrative examples

8 Interactive media production

P4 review strengths and weaknesses of own interactive media work	**M4** describe strengths and weaknesses of own interactive media work with some detail and with reference to appropriate illustrative examples	**D4** evaluate strengths and weaknesses of own interactive media work with reference to precise and detailed illustrative examples

9 Photography techniques

P3 review strengths and weaknesses of own photographic work	**M3** describe strengths and weaknesses of own photographic work with some detail and with reference to appropriate illustrative examples	**D3** evaluate strengths and weaknesses of own photographic work with reference to precise and detailed illustrative examples

How you will be assessed

Your skills in carrying out reviews that are well thought through will be targeted through an integrated production assignment or a separate targeted assignment, released after the post-production phase has been completed, in which you will review your completed work and the production process as a whole. Work submitted may be subject to sampling by your centre's External Verifier as part of Edexcel's ongoing quality assurance procedures.

Your assessment could be in the form of:

- a written assignment or review
- a presentation of results and findings
- an observation of a focus group.

James, Animation techniques

When I first started the course, I wondered how reviewing and evaluating my work would be relevant or necessary; I couldn't really see how it would help.

For my first animation production, I organised a viewing with my class and produced a kind of questionnaire for them to fill out. The questionnaire asked each individual what they thought of my product and how well it fitted my target audience (which, fortunately, they fitted into).

I was very surprised by the responses I got: it seemed that lots of people spotted little errors that we hadn't noticed during production and editing, and they all had really strong opinions on how the product should look and how effective the story was.

I found all of the feedback extremely helpful and it encouraged me to think about what I had done during the production process, how well I had managed my time and how effectively I had worked. It caused me to take a more critical look at my work, not only with the benefit of hindsight but also in terms of helping to think more about future projects.

I think a lot more about my audience and the quality and effectiveness of my product now and will always remember how blown away I was by people's comments the first time I got them. I really thought my product was excellent, but maybe I was too close to it to see where the problems might have been.

It just goes to show, everyone really is a critic!

- **How does James think that reviewing his work has helped him?**
- **What sort of reviews did he carry out?**
- **What does he identify as a reason for why he didn't see things that others saw?**

Reviewing

There are a number of different aspects to reviewing work and, although you are most likely to build in a review stage when you have completed your work, you will need to bear all of these in mind. In this section, we will look at:

- reviewing the production process
- reviewing your work against the audience expectations or customer requirements
- reviewing the finished product against initial ideas.

Reviewing the production process

For this stage of your evaluation, you can begin by conducting a review of production and post-production logs to gain a better understanding of the processes your group went through and to refresh your memory a little. Here you are looking at and analysing the process itself and not the actual product. Think about all of the good and bad things that have happened and subject them to analysis.

Pre–production, production and post–production

You will have developed your product using pre-production, production and post-production techniques as appropriate, all the time creating, implementing and referring to the relevant documentation. It is now time to go back to them and submit them to a review: give them a second, more critical look in the cold light of day and make some decisions about their fitness for purpose and how helpful they were to the production process.

The success of any media product depends on the audience's reactions to it. What do you need to think about when reviewing your media production?

Activity: Paperwork review

Gather together all of your paperwork and review it in a similar way to the review you carried out on your original idea. This time, you need to consider the following questions:

- How well have the documents been filled in?
- Are they clear and easy to follow or cluttered and hard to read?
- Are they all there and in the correct order?
- How often did you refer to them during the production process?
- Looking back over them, is there anything you can do to make them better working documents?

Make a note of the answers to these questions and keep in mind why they are being asked. In the future, you may find that you do things differently; you may become more meticulous in your processes.

Time management

Time management is an important aspect of everyday life and is particularly relevant during the production process as you will often be working to schedules and deadlines. Carry out the following task and then try to answer the questions listed below. Make a few notes on how time management affected your production.

1. Firstly, list your original scheduled completion dates for all phases of the production.

2. Now list the actual completion dates as detailed in your production diary.

   o How closely do these dates match?

   o Did any area of the production overrun and, if so, when and how?

   o What was the effect of missing your scheduled deadlines?

   o How did you manage your time to ensure any time lost was gained in a later phase?

How can missed deadlines have a negative impact on the success of your media product?

It is important to remember that in the creative media sector deadlines exist for a reason. All members of staff (cast, crew and so on) are being paid for their time and all of them have to use it productively. For example, overrunning on a film production can potentially cost millions of pounds in wages, as well as location and equipment costs, which may never be recouped through later sales. After all, the purpose of a production is to make it in the required time and within the required budget; it then needs to be marketed or sold in order to make money – it needs to be profitable.

Case study: Reviewing performance – Polly Campbell, Advertising executive

In my profession, we undertake work on many different projects that involve a team of people working together to ensure that our products are on the market at the right time. For example, seasonal releases, such as those at Christmas and summer, must be launched in time to maximise on a particular market.

Deadlines are of the utmost importance and sometimes you can get so focused on meeting them that silly mistakes are made or you fail to work as well with others as you would like. We therefore always carry out a 'lessons learned' review at the end of a project.

The lessons learned session allows us to reflect on the project as a whole and to all contribute our thoughts and ideas on how well we managed our time, resources and workload.

These reviews are extremely helpful and can often give us a great insight into what we can do differently the next time round in order to get things right and get the product out to the consumer as and when required, and with the minimum of complications.

- How will you structure a lessons learned session for one of your projects?

- How may different people react to feedback? How can you make this a positive experience?

- What will you do differently on your next project?

Technical competencies and creative abilities

For this part of the review process, you will need to look at the competencies of all team members, including yourself. At the beginning of the project, you would have allocated roles and it is likely that you would have done so by considering the strengths and weaknesses of the team members. It is the same in the professional creative media sector: people are hired to do certain jobs because of their skills and abilities, often as a result of the reputation they have built up over the years.

Whilst your team might have played to their strengths, that doesn't mean that everything went according to plan and you didn't experience problems along the way. Some group members might have had wonderfully creative ideas but these ideas turned out to be unrealistic or unworkable.

Use the following activity as a means of assessing the abilities of your group and how well they used their skills during the production process.

How many people were involved in your media production? How did you decide who took on each role?

Activity: Technical and creative review

Begin by making a list of the team members and the roles they carried out during the production. Next to each role, make a brief note of the technical or creative contribution it made to your work. For example, a camera operator can be seen as both a technical and a creative role, as they have to work the equipment as well as capture the director's ideas on camera.

Next, write your own mini review of each of the team members – including yourself – that analyses their technical and creative strengths and weaknesses throughout the production.

- Which team member was a good all-rounder?

- Did you find that people who you thought had strong technical abilities had difficulties working in their chosen area?

- Were there some unforeseen technical problems that had to be dealt with? If so, who worked best at overcoming these problems?

- Who had the most creative input on the production and were their ideas realised?

Team contribution

Here, you can look at the individual contributions made by members of your group and how they contributed to the final product. For example, if you worked on a video product, who was allocated the role of:

- director
- camera operator
- producer
- editor?

Some of your group might have been actors and some could have taken a production or technical role, however, the main job titles outlined here are the ones that possibly have the greatest effect on the look and content of a product.

The director should have ensured that the ideas in the script and storyboard were captured by the camera operator, who, in turn, should have used their skills and knowledge of camera techniques to frame and shoot the footage correctly. The producer should have planned and organised the production process and made sure that everybody had what they needed when they needed it. Finally, the editor should have taken the footage and transformed it into the final product you had originally hoped to produce, adding the sound, transitions, titles and effects.

Have things worked out like this for you? Possibly and possibly not; if not, then you need to look at why not. At this stage, it is important that you don't play the blame game and try to point the finger at any individual group member. For example, if the editing didn't work out as well as you had hoped, then why didn't it? Did the editor have enough help, guidance and assistance from the rest of the group? Was the paperwork sufficient and well filled out? Did you notice technical and aesthetic problems during the process and fail to do anything about them?

Evaluations are about analysis and commentary, and reflecting on what happened and its effects, so don't get personal or back away from the truth.

Finally, you need to consider your own contribution to the entire production process and how involved you have been with the work of the group as a whole. For this, you will probably need to review your production logs and other paperwork. Above all, you will need to be honest with yourself and truthful about what you have done over the past weeks.

When working in a group, you should focus on the big picture and try to cooperate with others at all time. You don't need to be a pushover, but you do need to respect the views, ideas and opinions of others; if you don't, then things can start to go wrong.

Case study: Jenny, Group leader for video production unit

When we began the video production unit and I found out that we would be working in groups, I couldn't wait to get started and was determined to be the team leader, to take charge and be in control!

I now realise that was the wrong attitude to have and the work we produced as a team has been affected as a result. There were a lot of strong characters in our group and we started to fall out over ideas right from the start. We also had someone in the group who was very unreliable and never turned up when we really needed them.

In the end, we cut that person out and tried to manage on our own, but there was too much to do and we fell behind. The disagreements got worse and I spent a lot of time feeling frustrated and wound up, which didn't help anybody.

As a result, our product didn't turn out the way we wanted it to. We didn't get the grade we had hoped for, so our individual contributions to the group worked against us.

- Why do you think there were issues within the group?
- What could have been done to resolve these issues?
- What do you think are the most important attributes to use when working in a group?

Were there any major disagreements between members of your group? How did you overcome these?

When analysing the work of your group – and remember, you are not just reflecting on your own contribution here – it is important to reflect on the input of each member in all areas of the production process.

- Were all group members active participants or did some lay back allowing others to do the work?

- Did anybody's actions result in something going right or wrong with the production?

- Was any particular group member a driving force behind the production?

- Did any one member display exceptional skills in a particular area of the process, such as editing or filming?

- How effective was the overall group dynamic and how beneficial was it to the process as a whole?

Remember to look at the positives as well as the negatives of the group roles and work undertaken; acknowledge individual contributions as well as the overall effectiveness of the group.

Reviewing to meet your audience or customer needs

Your target audience should have been kept in mind at all times throughout your production. After all, they are the consumer you are creating the product for and should be the driving force behind the production. Remember that in the creative media sector products are made for commercial purposes: they must make money and, therefore, they must sell to the required audience.

Go back over your work again and reflect on the original audience that you had identified for the product and the reasons why you thought that particular target group was appropriate.

1. Identify who the original audience was and why.

2. Reflect on the types of product this target audience consumes on a regular basis and think about the style and content of these products.

3. Now look at your final product and analyse its appropriateness. Does it fit in with the expectations of the intended audience?

If there have been changes and alterations to your product that have had an impact on its overall look, style or content, then you do need to seriously consider whether or not it is still going to suit your intended audience.

Focus groups are a very good source of feedback. Did you show your media product to a focus group during the production process?

Reviewing the finished product

The purpose of this section is to encourage you to think about your work retrospectively, looking back over your production and reviewing what you have done and how you did it. You can do this in many different ways, for example, you can discuss your final product with the rest of the group in which you are working to see what everybody thinks of it.

Another way can be to discuss the final product with your tutor. Your tutor may be able to give you some helpful feedback on the product's overall effectiveness, as well as what they have observed of your working practices.

If you have produced a film or audio product, you can show it to your class in order to gather an audience response to your final product and use that response to form the basis of part of your evaluation.

Whichever method you choose, you will need to write up a review of your final product, being analytical and evaluative at all times. This section outlines some different methods that you can use to gather information you can analyse and respond to.

Think about it

Completing post-production does not necessarily mean that your product is finished and ready for the audience; there may still be changes on the horizon as a result of audience feedback. Can you name any well-known products that have been altered as a result of such feedback?

Comparing with original proposal

When you set out to make your product, you should have had a clear idea as to what you wanted from it. You would have worked with your group to outline and form your ideas, which would have helped you to produce all of your planning documentation and, ultimately, to make your chosen product. The following activity will help you to reflect on your original concept and ideas, and start to think about how well you hit your targets.

Activity: Reviewing original ideas

Go right back to the start of the production process and gather together all of your original ideas and concepts. You will need your drafts, sketches, spidergrams, discussion notes and the final proposal document you drafted.

Go through your work in detail and make a note of what your original ideas were, picking out the details you felt were important at the time.

Now answer the following questions.

- What was the original product supposed to be?
- What genre did you choose to work in?
- What was the intended audience?
- How long did you want the product to be?
- What message were you trying to put across?
- How closely does your finished product match these original ideas? Be sure to make detailed notes of all the differences and why they occurred.

You might have thought you knew your ideas inside out, but you are now many weeks down the line from those original plans and your memory of them might have been affected by other factors. For example, you could have had filming and editing problems, causing you to change footage and, ultimately, your content. You might have found that your photographs did not look the way you had originally intended and you were unable to alter them sufficiently to suit your purposes.

Whatever the factors contributing to the changes, it is almost inevitable that changes would have been made. It is also possible that you might have just taken those changes to be part of your original idea and paid them little notice. This is why going back to the start and reflecting on your original ideas is helpful, allowing you to reflect on what you wanted and where you are now.

How have decisions you made during production and post-production affected your final product?

Technical and aesthetic qualities, style and content

How does your final product look and what is the overall technical quality? How do these affect the overall style and content of the final product?

Consider what in media terms is called the **aesthetic** or look of the product. This factor will affect all types of product, from print to video, as it is concerned with what the product looks like and whether it realises the original intentions. Reflect on the overall quality of the style and content of the product, and consider whether you have added all the necessary elements required for it to fit your chosen genre.

Whatever you set out for your product to look like, make sure that you managed to achieve this. If the purpose was to produce a glossy magazine and you have actually printed it out on dull, matt-finished paper then your product will not have the look you intended it to have.

Technical qualities are also a consideration. If you have produced a product that lacks technical competence then it is not going to fulfil its required intention. A programme that has been badly edited, with poor transitions and jumpy sound will neither look nor sound good and it will fail to get the message across as people will be too busy concentrating on the errors to pay attention to the content. If you have produced a web-based or interactive product, consider how easy it is to use and make sure that it works as intended, with no broken links for example.

Again, go through a checklist and make some decisions about your product. Be strong with yourself and be prepared to make some harsh judgments if you have to. Think about:

- the overall finish of the product
- the intended and actual look of the product
- the technical quality of the finished piece
- factors that contributed to changes in the final product
- what effect those changes have had on the product.

As an illustration, the following products have been created with an original idea and purpose in mind, but only one has finally realised its intentions in terms of all the required elements. Look over them and see whether you can identify which is which. Make a note of the things that are wrong and what you might have changed had you produced the work yourself.

What are the key differences between these two products?

Sources of information

There are many different areas of your work you can go back to in order to find the necessary information required to conduct your final evaluations. You will have your own memories of the process, as well as your class notes, and you should have produced some relevant and targeted documentation throughout. You can also look at other methods of gaining information on your product and processes, many of which have been outlined for you here.

Production log and documentation

Your production log should contain all of the technical and creative decisions you made throughout the production process. It should also contain details and commentary around production issues that might have arisen at certain times. You should have kept a detailed and concise summary of events that will allow you to reflect on the entire process and perform a useful evaluation of events.

It is also possible to reflect back on your production paperwork to see if it was changed or adapted during the process. Remember things like scripts and storyboards are working documents and it is possible that you or someone else might have made changes or written comments on these 'in situ' (in the appropriate place), which will give you an insight into what was happening at that particular time.

Comments from others

It is always vital to get feedback from others, as well as conducting your own review. This is because other people are not as close to the project as you are and, therefore, are more likely to see any faults or errors, or pick up on details you may have overlooked.

The audience of a product is always a good way to start and there can be different ways of getting them to review and feedback on your product. Some of the more technological means are outlined later in this section, but a current method used in the film industry is **test screening**. In these screenings, the audience is shown the film and asked to respond to what they see and how they feel about it. This feedback can then be analysed and changes made if and where necessary. The following case study reflects on how much impact this audience feedback can have.

Think about it

In the creative media sector, there are people who are paid to review media products and comment on them. Where might you find these reviewers? How do they make their commentaries available to the public? Can you name any famous film reviewers?

Case study: Test screenings – *Titanic*

It is reported that when director James Cameron's 1997 film *Titanic* was first shown at a test screening, the audience disliked a fight scene between the characters of Jack and Lovejoy, which took place after Jack and Rose escaped into the flooded dining room.

The scene had apparently been included to add suspense to the film. It featured Cal offering to give Lovejoy the Heart of the Ocean diamond if he could get it from Jack and Rose (although Cal had no intention of actually doing so). As a result, Lovejoy went after the pair into the sinking dining room. In revenge for earlier making it look like he'd stolen the necklace, Jack attacked Lovejoy.

Feedback from the test screening was that the audience thought it unrealistic to show someone risking their life purely for wealth. As a result, the scene was one of many to be cut from the final version.

- Cutting a scene may seem like an expensive waste of content that has cost time and money to produce. Besides the test audience's response to the scene, what other factors do you think played a part in James Cameron's decision to cut it?

- When scenes are cut from a video production, what impact can this have on continuity?

For your productions, it is likely that you will obtain feedback from your peers – in general, the other members of the class – as they are available to you and you can ask them to review your product and tell you what they think. Furthermore, they are likely to fit the profile of your intended target audience and, as a result, their feedback will be relevant and helpful.

You should also gain feedback from your tutors, who are likely to be acting as your client. They will have been the person responsible for commissioning your product in the first place and therefore what they think of it will be of the utmost importance! Make sure you are open to this feedback and the comments that may be made; don't get defensive or upset as this is not professional behaviour and will alienate you from your client or audience.

Questionnaire

For each question, please circle one option or write your answer in the space provided.

1. What is your gender?

    Male   **Female**

2. Which age range do you fall into?

    13–15   **16–18**   **19–21**   **22+**

3. What genre do you think this product is?

    _____

4. Do you usually consume products from this genre?

    Yes   **No**

5. Did you enjoy the product?

    Yes   **No**

6. Please explain in no more than two sentences which elements you liked best.

    _____
    _____
    _____
    _____
    _____

Thank you for your time.

Figure 9.1: What other questions would you like to ask your audience, to find out what they thought of your product?

New media formats

Modern technology means there are many methods available to you to catch the eye of your intended audience and to gain their feedback.

Blogs and forums are often used by media producers as a way of judging public opinion and reactions to products and services on offer. Sometimes existing blogs are accessed by media producers to gain information and other times new blogs are started by the producer as a way of inviting feedback.

Using these forms and techniques is particularly relevant to interactive products such as websites, as the user will have to be online in order to use your product in the first place. You can easily add a link to a blog and ask all new users to post commentary on it for you.

BTEC Assessment activity 9.1

When addressing these learning outcomes, you will be required to undertake evaluations of your work in your chosen area. Although you may have previously worked as part of a production team, you will be required to carry out your own evaluations of your final product.

The work for this learning outcome will be assessed by your tutor through observations of focus groups that you may hold and through submission of a written evaluation. This written evaluation should take into account all aspects of the product and its fitness for purpose, along with copies of your results and findings.

Using the methods outlined in this chapter, carry out a thorough review of your work looking in detail at the production process, team contributions and overall product. Identify the strengths and weaknesses of your work and be sure to use feedback from others to form your opinions.

Grading tips

To aim for a **merit**, you will need to make sure that your work takes the form of a discussion into what was good and effective, and what didn't work, using examples from your work to highlight your points.

To aim for a **distinction**, you will need to clearly explain and evaluate your product and what is good or bad about it using clear and detailed examples from your work to highlight and illustrate your points.

PLTS

Evaluating your experiences and learning to inform future progress, and inviting feedback on your own work, dealing positively with praise, setbacks and criticism, will help you to develop your skills as a **reflective learner**.

Functional skills

Presenting your findings as a result of feedback in a variety of different ways will help you to develop your **Mathematics** skills.

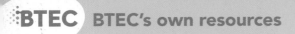

Learning outcomes

Unit	Name	Learning outcome
5	Video production	LO4 be able to review own video production work
6	Audio production	LO3 be able to review own audio production work
7	Print production	LO4 be able to review own print production work
8	Interactive media production	LO4 be able to review own interactive media production work
9	Photography techniques	LO3 be able to review own photography work
10	Animation techniques	LO4 be able to review own animation production
11	Web authoring	LO4 be able to review own web authoring work
12	Digital graphics for interactive and print-based media	LO3 be able to use digital tools to create digital graphics for interactive media products in response to a brief LO4 be able to use digital tools to create digital graphics for print media products in response to a brief
13	2D digital art for computer games	LO4 be able to use digital tools to create a 2D digital image and texture for a game from a concept drawing
18	Advertising production	LO4 be able to review own advertising production
19	Writing for the creative media	LO4 be able to review own writing work
20	Factual production for the creative media	LO4 be able to review own factual media production work
21	Creative media production project	LO4 be able to review own production project work

Simon Richardson
Marketing manager

Whatever the product or service, the best way to find out whether the marketing media, style and content is reaching and appealing to the right target audience is to test it. The cost of this can be high, so focus groups are called upon in advance of carrying out these tests. In the simplest terms, a focus group will contain potential or existing customers giving their opinion on either the existing product or service, or the concept of a new product or service.

The most formal scenario is for the focus group to sit behind a two-way mirror discussing the product while a moderator guides their conversation and hidden video cameras record them. The opposite extreme is to interview the target audience face to face in a one-to-one situation.

These exercises result in varying degrees of information, but we have found that having more people involved in the focus group gives a more accurate outcome.

A common scenario is for the focus group of a marketing campaign to look at the marketing piece and critique it.

For example, a direct mail piece from a supermarket had a very specific format that had provided exceptional results for a number of years. When response started to dip, a focus group of previous recipients was called upon for their feedback. The views collected included comments about the amount of information given on the size of the marketing piece. This information was then fed through to the creative department. As a result, the designers could create new concepts to show the focus group, prior to production taking place.

In this way, we are able to step back and look at the products and services being provided and analyse their effectiveness, how competitive they are, whether they are cost-effective and whether they are hitting the right target market.

Think about it

1. Why does this marketing company use focus groups?
2. What sort of products do they ask the groups to review?
3. How effective are these groups in providing information on existing products?
4. What action can the company take as a result of the consumer feedback?

Just checking

1. What are the areas you should consider when reviewing your final product?
2. Why are all of these considerations important to your evaluations?
3. When looking at your team contribution, what do you feel is the most important factor to consider?
4. When looking at your individual contribution, what do you think is the most important factor to consider?
5. How much help do you think well-prepared and maintained planning documents will be to the review process?
6. How will you evaluate the time management on your production?
7. How is the reviewing process used by professionals in the creative media sector?
8. Why is the review process so important to the creative media sector?
9. What is a focus group and how are they used in the creative media sector?
10. Can you name any occasions when the review process has changed the final outcome of a creative media product?

Assignment tips

- When asking for feedback on your product, you must make sure that you have structured questions to ask.
- You can provide the viewer with a questionnaire asking them about specific areas of your product. You can also ask them to provide written or even verbal feedback. Whatever form you use, remember to maintain a **focus** at all times: what do you want to know and why do you want to know it?
- Never use the review process to outline what you have done during a project. By all means, refer to specific areas or processes, but don't just explain what you did – that is not evaluation.
- Remember to comment on what went well as well as what didn't. You need to show that you are aware of the strengths and the weaknesses of your production.
- Check your written content before you hand it in. Does it make sense? Have you made the best use of the feedback you obtained?
- As a final check, why not ask someone else to review your review? They may have something else to add that you never even thought about.

Assessment and grading criteria

Investigation

The table below shows you the relevant grading criteria for further optional units with an investigation element.

To achieve a **pass** grade the evidence must show that you are able to:	To achieve a **merit** grade the evidence must show that, in addition to the pass criteria, you are able to:	To achieve a **distinction** grade the evidence must show that, in addition to the pass and merit criteria, you are able to:
12 Digital graphics for interactive and print-based media		
P1 outline the key characteristics of digital graphics technology	**M1** describe digital graphics technology with some detail and with reference to appropriate illustrative examples	**D1** explain digital graphics technology with reference to precise and detailed examples, using correct technical language
13 2D digital art for computer games		
P1 outline the key characteristics of digital graphics technology	**M1** describe digital graphics technology with some detail and with reference to appropriate illustrative examples	**D1** explain digital graphics technology with reference to precise and detailed illustrative examples and using correct technical language
P2 outline graphic styles and graphical themes used in games	**M2** describe graphic styles and graphical themes used in games with some detail and with reference to appropriate illustrative examples	**D2** explain graphic styles and graphical themes used in games with reference to precise and detailed illustrative examples and using correct technical language
14 Deconstructing computer games		
P1 outline the development and capabilities of computer game platforms	**M1** describe the development and capabilities of computer game platforms with some detail and with reference to appropriate illustrative examples	**D1** explain the development and capabilities of computer game platforms with reference to precise and detailed illustrative examples
P2 outline the features of computer game components	**M2** describe computer game components with some detail and with some reference to appropriate illustrative examples	**D2** explain computer game components with reference to precise and detailed illustrative examples

15 Computer games testing

P1 outline the game development process	**M1** describe the development process with some detail and with reference to appropriate illustrative examples	**D1** explain the game development process with reference to precise and detailed illustrative examples
P2 outline the phases of game testing	**M2** describe the phases of game testing with some detail and with reference to appropriate illustrative examples	**D2** explain the phases of game testing with reference to precise and detailed illustrative examples
P3 outline defect types found within games	**M3** describe defect types found within games with some detail and with reference to appropriate illustrative examples	**D3** explain defect types found within games with reference to precise and detailed illustrative examples

16 2D computer game engines

P1 outline the features of 2D game platforms and their limitations	**M1** describe 2D game platforms and their limitations with some detail and with reference to appropriate illustrative examples	**D1** explain 2D game platforms and their limitations with reference to precise and detailed illustrative examples and using correct technical language
P2 outline graphic, behavioural and sound 2D game assets	**M2** describe graphic, behavioural and sound 2D game assets with some detail and with reference to appropriate illustrative examples	**D2** explain graphic, behavioural and sound 2D game assets with reference to precise and detailed illustrative examples and using correct technical language
P3 outline how 2D game engines are used to build a game world	**M3** describe how 2D game engines are used to build a game world with some detail and with reference to appropriate illustrative examples	**D3** explain how 2D game engines are used to build a game world with reference to precise and detailed illustrative examples and using correct technical language

17 3D computer game engines

P1 outline the features of 3D game platforms and their connectable devices	**M1** describe the features of 3D game platforms and their connectable devices with some detail and with reference to appropriate illustrative examples	**D1** explain the features of 3D game platforms and their connectable devices with reference to precise and detailed illustrative examples and using correct technical language
P2 outline graphic, behavioural and sound 3D game assets	**M2** describe graphic, behavioural and sound 3D game assets with some detail and with reference to appropriate illustrative examples	**D2** explain graphic, behavioural and sound 3D game assets with reference to precise and detailed illustrative examples and using correct technical language
P3 outline how 3D game engines are used to build a game world	**M3** describe how 3D game engines are used to build a game world with some detail and with reference to appropriate illustrative examples	**D3** explain how 3D game engines are used to build a game world with reference to precise and detailed illustrative examples and using correct technical language

18 Advertising production

P1 outline advertisements in terms of content, style and technique	**M1** describe advertisements in terms of content, style and technique with some detail and with reference to appropriate illustrative examples	**D1** explain advertisements in terms of content, style and technique with reference to precise and detailed illustrative examples

19 Writing for the creative media

P1 outline different types of writing produced in the creative media sector	**M1** describe different types of writing produced in the creative media sector with some detail and with reference to appropriate illustrative examples	**D1** evaluate different types of writing produced in the creative media sector with reference to precise and detailed illustrative examples

20 Factual production for the creative media

P1 outline the conventions of factual media formats	**M1** describe the conventions of factual media formats with some detail and with reference to appropriate illustrative examples	**D1** evaluate conventions of factual media formats with reference to precise and detailed illustrative examples

Pre-production

The table below shows you the relevant grading criteria for further optional units with a pre-production element.

To achieve a **pass** grade the evidence must show that you are able to:	To achieve a **merit** grade the evidence must show that, in addition to the pass criteria, you are able to:	To achieve a **distinction** grade the evidence must show that, in addition to the pass and merit criteria, you are able to:
13 2D digital art for computer games		
P3 apply appropriate pencil drawing techniques to create concept art for a game, partially realising intentions	**M3** apply appropriate pencil drawing techniques competently to create concept art for a game, mainly realising intentions	**D3** apply appropriate pencil drawing techniques skilfully and imaginatively to create concept art for a game, clearly realising intentions
16 2D computer game engines		
P4 apply tools and features of a 2D game engine to build, to a specification, a playable game world that partially realises intentions	**M4** apply tools and features of a 2D game engine competently to build, to a specification, a playable game world that mainly realises intentions	**D4** apply tools and features of a 2D game engine skilfully to build, to a specification, a playable game world that clearly realises intentions
17 3D computer game engines		
P4 apply tools and features of a 3D game engine to build, to a specification, a playable game world that partially realises intentions	**M4** apply tools and features of a 3D game engine competently to build, to a specification, a playable game world that mainly realises intentions	**D4** apply tools and features of a 3D game engine skilfully to build, to a specification, a playable game world that clearly realises intentions
18 Advertising production		
P2 present an appropriate idea for an advertisement	**M2** present a developed idea for an advertisement	**D2** present an imaginative idea for an advertisement
19 Writing for the creative media		
P2 present appropriate ideas for written material	**M2** present developed ideas for written material	**D2** present imaginative ideas for written material
20 Factual production for the creative media		
P2 present ideas for a factual media product	**M2** present developed ideas for a factual product	**D2** present well-developed and imaginative ideas for a factual media product

21 Creative media production project

P1 prepare a written proposal for a media product	**M1** prepare a developed written proposal for a media product	**D1** prepare and imaginative and well-detailed written proposal for a media product
P2 complete pre-production for a proposed media product	**M2** complete pre-production for a proposed media product competently	**D2** complete pre-production for a proposed media product thoroughly

Production

The table below shows you the relevant grading criteria for further optional units with a production element.

To achieve a **pass** grade the evidence must show that you are able to:	To achieve a **merit** grade the evidence must show that, in addition to the pass criteria, you are able to:	To achieve a **distinction** grade the evidence must show that, in addition to the pass and merit criteria, you are able to:
11 Web authoring		
P3 use web authoring software to create a website that partially realises intentions	**M3** use web authoring software competently to create a website that mainly realises intentions	**D3** use web authoring software skilfully to create a website that clearly realises intentions
16 2D computer game engines		
P4 apply tools and features of a 2D game engine to build, to a specification, a playable game world that partially realises intentions	**M4** apply tools and features of a 2D game engine competently to build, to a specification, a playable game world that mainly realises intentions	**D4** apply tools and features of a 2D game engine skilfully to build, to a specification, a playable game world that clearly realises intentions
17 3D computer game engines		
P4 apply tools and features of a 3D game engine to build, to a specification, a playable game world that partially realises intentions	**M4** apply tools and features of a 3D game engine competently to build, to a specification, a playable game world that mainly realises intentions	**D4** apply tools and features of a 3D game engine skilfully to build, to a specification, a playable game world that clearly realises intentions
18 Advertising production		
P3 use appropriate techniques and technology to create an advertisement that partially realises intentions	**M3** use appropriate techniques and technology competently to create an advertisement that mainly realises intentions	**D3** use appropriate techniques and technology skilfully to create an advertisement that clearly realises intentions
19 Writing for the creative media		
P3 apply conventions and technical skills to produce written material that partially realises intentions	**M3** apply conventions competently and technical skills with some accuracy to produce written material that mainly realises intentions	**D3** apply conventions skilfully and technical skills accurately to produce written material that clearly realises intentions
20 Factual production for the creative media		
P3 apply appropriate conventions and use appropriate technology to create a factual media product that partially realises intentions	**M3** apply appropriate conventions and use appropriate technology competently to create a factual media product that mainly realises intentions	**D3** apply appropriate conventions and use appropriate technology skilfully to create a factual media product that clearly realises intentions

21 Creative media production project

P3 apply appropriate technology and techniques to create a proposed media product that partially realises intentions	**M3** apply appropriate conventions and use appropriate technology competently to create a proposed media product that mainly realises intentions	**D3** apply appropriate conventions and use appropriate technology skilfully to create a proposed media product that clearly realises intentions

Review

The table below shows you the relevant grading criteria for further optional units with a review element.

To achieve a **pass** grade the evidence must show that you are able to:	To achieve a **merit** grade the evidence must show that, in addition to the pass criteria, you are able to:	To achieve a **distinction** grade the evidence must show that, in addition to the pass and merit criteria, you are able to:
10 Animation techniques		
P4 review strengths and weaknesses of own animation production work	**M4** describe strengths and weaknesses of own animation production work with some detail and with reference to appropriate illustrative examples	**D4** evaluate strengths and weaknesses of own animation production work with reference to precise and detailed illustrative examples
11 Web authoring		
P4 review strengths and weaknesses of own web authoring work	**M4** describe strengths and weaknesses of own web authoring work with some detail and with reference to appropriate illustrative examples	**D4** evaluate strengths and weaknesses of own web authoring work with reference to precise and detailed illustrative examples
12 Digital graphics for interactive and print-based media		
P3 apply appropriate digital graphics tools to create, in response to a brief, digital graphic images for interactive media products, partially realising intentions	**M3** apply digital graphics tools competently to create, in response to a brief, digital graphic images for interactive media products, mainly realising intentions	**D3** apply digital graphics tools skilfully and imaginatively to create, in response to a brief, digital graphic images for interactive media products, clearly realising intentions
P4 apply appropriate digital graphics tools to create, in response to a brief, digital graphic images for print media products, partially realising intentions	**M4** apply digital graphics tools competently to create, in response to a brief, digital graphic images for print media products, mainly realising intentions	**D4** apply digital graphics tools skilfully and imaginatively to create, in response to a brief, digital graphic images for print media products, clearly realising intentions
13 2D digital art for computer games		
P4 apply appropriate digital graphics tools to create a 2D digital image and texture for a game from a concept drawing, partially realising intentions	**M4** apply appropriate digital graphics tools competently to create a 2D digital image and texture for a game from a concept drawing, mainly realising intentions	**D4** apply appropriate digital graphics tools skilfully and imaginatively to create a 2D digital image and texture for a game from a concept drawing, clearly realising intentions

18 Advertising production

P4 review strengths and weaknesses of own advertising production work

M4 describe strengths and weaknesses of own advertising production work with some detail and with reference to appropriate illustrative examples

D4 evaluate strengths and weaknesses of own advertising production work with reference to precise and detailed illustrative examples

19 Writing for the creative media

P4 review strengths and weaknesses of own writing work

M4 describe strengths and weaknesses of own writing work with some detail and with reference to appropriate illustrative examples

D4 evaluate strengths and weaknesses of own work with reference to precise and detailed illustrative examples

20 Factual production for the creative media

P4 review strengths and weaknesses of own factual media production work

M4 describe strengths and weaknesses of own factual media production work with some detail and with reference to appropriate illustrative examples

D4 evaluate strengths and weaknesses of factual media production work with reference to precise and detailed illustrative examples

21 Creative media production project

P4 review strengths and weakness of own production project work

M4 describe strengths and weaknesses of own production project work with some detail and with reference to appropriate illustrative examples

D4 evaluate strengths and weaknesses of own production project work with reference to precise and detailed illustrative examples

Industry fact files

The Creative Media Production sector includes many industries, each with a wide range of roles. Here are some fact files about people who work in different parts of the Creative Media Production sector.

John Whittaker, Moderator

Focus group moderator at The Oxford Research Agency

Job role:
- Focus groups are used to obtain qualitative data about a subject or product from a group of people representing the target audience.
- The moderator engages with the members of the focus group and persuades them to open up and reveal their true opinions.
- The moderator will be provided with a discussion guide, outlining what the client is hoping to find out from the focus group. However, this is only a guide: the moderator must react to what respondents are (and are not saying), and to their body language, to allow the discussion to flow naturally.

Key skills needed for job:
- Good communication skills.
- An ability to engage with members of the focus group and persuade them to open up and give their true opinions.
- A flexible approach and the ability to react to what members of the focus group are saying and guide the conversation so that it stays on track.
- Preparation skills - the moderator must be fully aware of what the client wants to find out.

Industry buzz words: dynamic, exciting.

Alastair Williams, Creative Director

Creative Director at Mark Making (a creative agency)

Job role:
- Clients come to the creative agency with a particular communication challenge (a brief). The creative team in the studio comes up with various ideas for the brief, which Alastair then presents to the client.
- Presentations to the client must be clear and convincing. Presentation style will depend on the client, but may involve use of an overhead projector, a PowerPoint presentation, or boards showing samples of the work the company could produce.

Key skills needed for job:
- Good communication skills, both written and spoken.
- Good presentation skills, and the ability to tailor the tone and style of presentations to suit different clients.
- Good listening skills, and the ability to understand and interpret clients' needs.
- Enthusiasm for your work: the client must feel that you care about their product.

Industry buzz words: creativity, enthusiasm, innovation.

Stuart Cox, professional freelance photographer

Job role:
- Stuart meets the client so they can talk through to ensure he has a thorough understanding of what they want him to shoot and how. Most clients will produce a mood board and a detailed brief, and Stuart will let them know exactly what is (or is not) technically possible.
- Some clients will send an art director or producer on the shoot, to ensure that the brief is met. Stuart will work with this director or producer to overcome any challenges encountered on the shoot.
- After the shoot, Stuart presents the client with a disc or an online selection of low resolution images. The client will look through this selection, chooses which images they wish to develop further, and let Stuart know of any changes or retouching they would like him to make. Stuart will then produce the images, making any necessary changes, and deliver the final, high resolution, product to the client.

Key skills needed for job:
- Flexibility – you need to be able to adapt your style to meet client needs; to be able to work around challenges as you encounter them.
- Willingness to learn new skills and experiment with new ways of working so that your work remains fresh and interesting.
- Good listening skills, and the ability to understand and interpret clients' ideas.
- Good technical knowledge of what is and is not possible within your working parameters (e.g. studio location, subject matter, etc.).
- Good team working skills: it may be necessary to work with an art director sent by the client to ensure the brief is met.

Industry buzz words: competitive, changeable, exciting.

David Hunt, Chief Technology Officer

Chief Technology Officer (CTO) at Lightning Fish (a games developer)

Job role:
- David is a programmer, who manages the technology in the company.
- During the design and development process, he studies other people's products to see what types of features they include, how they work, and whether it would be worth including similar features in a new game.
- David is also involved in tailoring new products to suit the various different games platforms and gaming hardware.

Key skills needed for job:
- Good understanding of the market, so you can work out what will sell in order to tailor your products to meet market needs or wants.
- Good presentation skills, so you can sell your ideas to a publisher who will fund and market your product.
- An ability to compromise: more ambitious ideas may not be feasible within time and budget constraints.
- Creativity – the games market is highly competitive, so you will need to come up with new ideas, or a fresh take on an existing product.
- Good technical knowledge of the computer programs you are working with and the games consoles you are designing your products for, so that you know what is possible.

Industry buzz words: fast-moving, competitive.

Richard Healey, Television producer / director

Television producer / director at ITV (a television channel)

Job role:
- During pre-production, the producer/director:
  - develops ideas
  - decides on locations for filming
  - produces a script
  - casts actors/presenters
  - produces a production schedule and a call sheet
  - completes a risk assessment for every location etc.
  - produces storyboards, shot lists, camera plans etc.
  - produces a demonstrable plan of action
  - obtains all relevant permissions and permits
  - develops contingency plans, in case anything goes wrong.
- The producer/director is also involved in production and post-production work.

Key skills needed for job:
- Good organisational skills.
- Ability to complete all documentation – before work begins the following must be completed: production schedules, call sheets, risk assessments, permissions documentation, etc.
- An ability to think logically and plan your work carefully.
- The capacity to be flexible and produce contingency plans if necessary.

Industry buzz words: complex, detailed, well-organised.

Simon Clayton, Designer

Designer (mainly web and some print design) at Simon Clayton Design

Job role:
- After the designer has received a brief from a client, the first step in the design process is to produce a 'wire frame' for the site. This allows the designer to come with ideas for the site, in terms of page layout, navigation and so on.
- Once the wire frame is competed, the site can be 'populated' – text and images will be added in and a working 'Beta' version of the site will be presented to the client for approval. If the client has any suggestions or requests for changes, these will be built into the final version of the site.
- For larger projects, it may be necessary to bring in programmers (e.g. specialists in Java script, PHP etc.), illustrators, photographers, copy writers or other specialists.
- The designer must also consider accessibility: font sizes, image sizes, clickable areas etc.

Key skills needed for job:
- Good team-working skills: web design is likely to involve various specialists
- Good listening skills, and the ability to understand and interpret the needs of both clients and users of the website
- Good technical knowledge of the various software programs you may be using, and an ability to tailor your website to suit different computer systems

Industry buzz words: innovative, forward thinking.

James Heinz, Re-recording mixer

Re-recording mixer (sound post-production) for film and television productions

Job role:
- Once the picture for a film or television programme has been locked, the picture editor will produce an OMF file which will be handed over the sound editors.
- The director will meet with the sound supervisor and the sound editor to discuss which dialogue needs to be replaced and where sound effects should be added.
- A dialogue editor will 'clean up' the dialogue (removing breath sounds, clicks etc.) and an effects editor will add background noise atmosphere and spot effects (dog barks, car passes etc.). Once the dialogue and effects editors have finished, the re-recording mixer will balance the dialogue and sound effects, working with the director and producer to decide on the sound design for each scene.
- Once the soundtrack has been edited, the re-recording mixer must produce 'deliverables' – separate tracks for dialogue, music and sound effects. This means that the film can be re-dubbed into any language by replacing the language track only: the music and sound effects will be unchanged.

Key skills needed for job:
- Good listening skills.
- The ability to:
  o hear and edit music and other sound effects
  o balance dialogue, sound effects and music to achieve the desired effect or create a certain mood or atmosphere
  o understand and interpret the vision of the director and producer.
- Good technical knowledge of editing software.

Industry buzz words: interesting, exciting.

Ask your tutor about extra materials to help you through your course. They will be able to provide you with interesting videos, activities, presentations and information about the Creative Media Production sector.

Glossary

Agenda – a list of the items that are to be covered in a specific meeting, together with the date, time and location of the meeting.

Analogue – an older and soon to be outdated system of broadcast and data transfer.

AOB – agenda item that stands for 'any other business'.

Bibliography – a list of books that you have used in your research project.

Code – a set of elements and characteristics that generate meaning for the audience.

Codes and conventions – a set of elements and characteristics that help to define a particular type of media product.

Content analysis – the study of the content of a media product. It produces quantifiable data and involves counting particular elements or features within the product.

Continuity – the maintenance of consistent detail in the scenes of a video production.

Creative media sector – includes all areas of media production, from traditional to interactive media.

Creative skills – skills required to generate ideas and concepts in order to create media products.

Demographics – the study of people according to factors like age, gender and ethnicity.

Digital – the editing system currently used in the industry.

Genre – French word meaning 'type'.

Geodemographics – the study of people based on where they live.

Iconography – how visual images within a media text can generate meaning.

Industry sectors – the different parts of the media industry categorised by their type of output, for example, television, film, radio and print.

Mass market – a large target audience that is not very well defined or segmented.

Media consumer – somebody who watches, listens to, reads or interacts with a media product.

Memo – short for 'memorandum', a memo is a brief note with details of things to be done or remembered.

Minutes – a written summary of who was at a meeting, what was said and what actions were agreed.

Mise-en-scène – the elements put in front of the camera to be filmed.

Mode of address – the way in which a media product communicates to its audience.

Niche market – a small, well-defined, specialised target audience.

Pitch – a presentation in which you try to sell your idea for a media production to a potential client.

Primary research – original research to obtain new information using techniques such as interviews, questionnaires and focus groups.

Production documentation – documentation covering all production paperwork from pre-production to post-production.

Production software – software used to create a presentation.

Profile – a set of information that summarises what a person is like.

Progressive web standards – using the most up-to-date usability and accessibility standards and guidelines available at the time of production.

Proposal – a document that explains your idea to a potential client or customer.

Prototype – a working model that can be used to test the visual design, technical functionality and user experience.

Psychographics – the study of people based on their attitudes, opinions and lifestyle.

Qualitative research – research that is based on opinions, attitudes and preferences, rather than facts and figures.

Quantitative research – research based on measurable facts and information that can be counted, producing numerical and statistical data.

Reading a text – a term used within the creative media sector to mean consuming and making sense of a media product.

Recce – a visit to a potential location to check out its suitability for recording your product.

Rendering – rendering should not be done until the end of the editing process; this is because rendered footage cannot be altered.

Secondary research – research using information already gathered by other people or organisations. Often available in books, magazines or websites.

Structure – how a company or industry is organised.

SWOT analysis – a simple tool to assess the strengths and weaknesses of an idea, as well as the opportunities that it will bring and the potential threats.

Technical skills – skills and knowledge needed to operate and work with technical equipment such as in a radio studio.

Timeline – the view of your product that will be provided at the bottom of the screen when using footage capture software during audio-visual post-production.

Titles – during audio-visual post-production, these can be added anywhere within your footage but are always required at the start and finish.

Transitions (audio-visual post-production) – also known as cuts, fades, wipes and so on; allow for a smoother 'transition' between clips.

Transitions (presentations) – devices used to add a flourish to a presentation when moving from one slide/screen to the next.

Treatment – the initial outline of your proposed production, providing details of scenes, characters and locations.

Trimming – the process by which you cut down your chosen clips.

Visual aid – a device used to make your presentation more visually appealing, for example handouts, clipart, video clips, charts, graphs and screen shots.

Wireframes – detailed sketches showing the types of content and on-screen position of assets. These can be created in presentation or drawing software programs.

Working practices – professional practices and conduct within the creative media sector.

Index

2D computer game engines
    grading criteria 122, 142, 213
    learning outcomes 118
2D digital art for computer games
    grading criteria 106, 122, 216
    learning outcomes 118
3D computer game engines
    grading criteria 122, 142, 213
    learning outcomes 118

A
accessibility standards 166
advertising production
    grading criteria 122, 172, 213, 215,
        216
    investigation of 113
    learning outcomes 118
    post-production 187
adverts for jobs 73–4
age of audience 13–14
agendas 125
analogue 174
animation techniques
    grading criteria 106, 122, 142, 172,
        192
    learning outcomes 118
AOB 125
as-live recordings 154, 157
assessment criteria
    audiences, media 78
    communication skills 28
    creative media sector 54
    investigation 106
    optional units 106
    post-production 172
    pre-production 122
    production process 142
    products, media 78
    research 2
    reviews 192
assignment tips
    audiences 104
    communication skills 52
    creative media sector 76
    investigation 120
    pre-production 140
    production process 170
    products, media 104
    research 26
    reviews 210
audiences
    assessment criteria 78
    assignment tips 104
    classification of 13–15, 81–3
    construction of products for
        specific 88–97
    feedback from 205–6
    functional skills 84, 87

grading criteria 78
grading tips 97, 102
identifying 80–7
interaction with 40
modes of address 90–1
personal, learning and thinking skills
    (PLTS) 84, 87
for presentations 39
research into 85–7
responses to media products 98–102
reviewing suitability of product for
    200
audio production
    as-live recordings 154
    editing 182
    grading criteria 106, 142, 172, 192
    interviews 154
    learning outcomes 118
    links and idents 182–3
    live recordings and
        entertainment 153–5
    production process 151–7
    production schedule 153–7157
    recording/editing formats 151, 153–7
    sound effects 155
audio-visual editing 174–80

B
BBC News Centre 88
bibliography 21
body language 42
Broadcasters' Audience Research
    Board 85–6

C
careers in creative media sector 62–4
    job adverts 73–4
    progression routes 71
    self appraisal 73
    skills and qualifications 70–1
    transferable skills 72
classification of audiences 81–3
closed narrative 91
codes 99–101
codes and conventions 92–3
codes of practice and conduct 62, 65–6
communication skills
    assessment criteria 28
    assignment tips 52
    discussions 30–1
    functional skills 36, 43, 50
    grading criteria 28
    grading tips 36, 43, 50
    interaction with others 33–6
    oral 32–3
    personal, learning and thinking skills
        (PLTS) 36, 43, 50
    presentations 20–4, 37–42

vocabulary 47–8
written 44–9
computer games testing
    grading criteria 213
    learning outcomes 118
conditions of work 67–9
constraints on media products 93–7
content analysis 109–10
continuity 151
contracts 67–8
copyright 37, 93, 163
creative media production project 214,
    215, 216
    see also post-production; pre-
        production; production process
creative media sector
    assessment criteria 54
    assignment tips 76
    conditions of work 67–9
    contracts 67–9
    flexibility in 67–9
    functional skills 69, 74
    grading criteria 54
    grading tips 61, 69, 74
    industries in 57
    jobs in 58, 62–4
    personal, learning and thinking skills
        (PLTS) 61, 69, 74
    size of organizations 59–60
    working hours limits 67
creative skills 62, 63, 64
creative thinker 137
cross-media formats 59
cross-media producers 59
culture of audience 14
cuts 180

D
data protection 93
Data Protection Act 11
deconstructing computer games
    grading criteria 106
    learning outcomes 118
defamation 93
deliverables 163
demographics 82
digital graphics
    grading criteria 106, 122, 216
    learning outcomes 118
digital media production
    deliverables 163
    production cycle 164
    production process 162–6
    sourcing graphics and images 163
    testing 165
directors 64
discussions 30–1
documentation 44–9

E

edit decision list 177
editing formats 151, 174–80, 182
editorial skills 63, 64
editors 64
efficiency 72
employment in creative media sector
  conditions of work 67–9
  job adverts 73–4
  job roles 58, 62–4
  progression routes 71
  self appraisal 73
  skills and qualifications for 70–1
  transferable skills 72
  working hours limits 67
English 5, 36, 50, 84, 117, 137, 167
equipment during pre-production 130
essays 47
evaluation. see reviews
expression, clarity of 33
eye contact 41

F

factual production for the creative media
  grading criteria 172, 213, 214, 215,
    216
  learning outcomes 118
  post-production 187
fades 180
feedback on products 205
Film London 129
film promotion 64
financial skills 63, 64
FireWire 179–80
flexibility of contracts 67–9
floor managers 64
focus groups 5
functional skills
  audiences 87
  communication skills 43, 50
  creative media sector 69, 74
  English 5, 36, 50, 84, 117, 137, 167
  ICT 17, 19, 24, 61, 69, 74, 97, 149,
    188
  investigation 117
  Mathematics 43
  post-production 188
  pre-production 137
  presentations 24
  production process 149, 167
  products, media 84, 87, 97
  research 5, 17, 19, 24

G

gender of audience 14
generic codes 99–101
genre 91, 92–3
geodemographics 82
grading criteria
  2D computer game engines 122, 142,
    213

2D digital art for computer
    games 106, 122, 216
3D computer game engines 122, 142,
    213
advertising production 122, 172, 213,
    216
animation techniques 106, 122, 142,
    172, 192
audio production 106, 142, 172, 192
communication skills 28
computer games testing 213
creative media production
    project 215, 216
creative media sector 54
deconstructing computer games 106
digital graphics 106, 122, 216
factual production for the creative
    media 172, 213, 214, 215, 216
interactive media production 106,
    122, 142, 192
investigation 106
optional units 106, 122, 142, 192,
    213–15, 215
photography techniques 122, 142,
    172, 192
post-production 172
pre-production 122
print production 106, 122, 142, 192
production process 142, 215
products, media 78
research 2
reviews 192, 216
video production 122, 142, 172, 192
web authoring 106, 122, 192
writing for the creative media 213,
    214, 215
grading tips
  audiences 87, 97, 102
  communication skills 36, 43, 50
  creative media sector 61, 69, 74
  investigation 117
  post-production 188
  pre-production 137, 214
  presentations 43
  production process 167
  products, media 87, 97, 102
  research 11, 19
  reviews 207
graphics, sourcing 163
group roles and responsibilities 144–6

H

hazards, identifying 147–9
health and safety 127, 146–9

I

iconography 101
ICT skills 17, 19, 24, 61, 97, 149
ideas
  choosing 126
  developing 127–30
  generation of 124–5

idents 182–3
images
  manipulation of 184–6
  sourcing 163
independent enquirers 17, 50, 61, 69,
    97, 117
industry sectors 56, 57
intellectual property 163
interaction with others 33–6
interactive media production
  grading criteria 106, 122, 142, 192
  investigation of 114
  learning outcomes 118
interviews 109, 154
investigation
  assessment criteria 106
  assignment tips 120
  functional skills 117
  grading criteria 106
  grading tips 117
  learning outcomes 118
  optional units 106, 213
  personal, learning and thinking skills
    (PLTS) 117
  presentation of results 115–17
  primary research 108–10
  purpose of 111–14
  secondary research 111

J

jobs in creative media sector 62–4
  job adverts 73–4
  progression routes 71
  skills and qualifications 70–1
  transferable skills 72

K

Knightley, Keira 94

L

language codes 99
learning outcomes
  investigation 118
  optional units 118, 138, 168, 208
  pre-production 138
  production process 168
  reviews 208
libel law 94
lifestyle of audiences 82
linear editing 174–5
links and idents 182–3
live recordings and entertainment 153–5
location of audiences 82–3

M

managerial skills 63, 64
marketing 63
mass market 81
Mathematics 43
meetings 30–1, 125
memos 45
microphones 151

minutes 45, 125
mise-en-scène 101
modes of address 90–1
multimedia conglomerates 59
multi-strand narrative 91

N

narrative structure 91
newspaper editors 64
niche markets 81
non-linear editing 175–6

O

observation 108
open narrative 91
optional units
   assessment criteria 106
   grading criteria 106, 122, 142, 192, 213–15
   investigation 106, 213
   learning outcomes 138, 208
   pre-production 122, 214
   production process 142, 215
   reviews 192, 216
oral communication 32–3, 116

P

paperwork
   during pre-production 131–4
   video production 150
pay in the creative media sector 69
permissions 129
personal, learning and thinking skills (PLTS)
   audiences 87
   communication skills 36, 43, 50
   creative media sector 61, 69, 74
   creative thinkers 19, 137
   independent enquirers 17, 50, 61, 69, 74, 97, 117
   investigation 117
   post-production 188
   pre-production 137
   presentations 24
   production process 149, 167
   products, media 84, 97
   reflective learners 24, 36, 43, 207
   research 5, 17, 19, 24
   reviews 207
   self-managers 167, 188
   team workers 5, 84
personal attributes 72
photography techniques
   finishing and placement 186
   grading criteria 122, 142, 172, 192
   image manipulation 184–6
   post-production 184–6
pitches 37, 136
post-production
   advertising production 187
   assessment criteria 172
   assignment tips 190

audio-visual editing 174–80
   edit decision list 177
   editing formats 174–6
   factual production for the creative media 187
   functional skills 188
   grading criteria 172
   grading tips 188
   personal, learning and thinking skills (PLTS) 188
   photography techniques 184–6
   radio production 181–3
   reviews 194–5
pre-production
   assessment criteria 122
   assignment tips 140
   choosing an idea 126–7
   developing ideas 127–30
   equipment 130
   functional skills 137
   grading criteria 122
   grading tips 137, 214
   idea generation 124–5
   learning outcomes 138
   optional units 122, 214
   paperwork 131–4
   permissions 129
   personal, learning and thinking skills (PLTS) 137
   presentation of ideas 136–7
   proposals 126, 135
   research 127–8
   reviews 194–5
   test shoots and recordings 130
presentations
   during 41
   audience 39–40
   copyright 37, 115
   grading tips 43
   of ideas during pre-production 136–7
   preparation for 41
   of research results 20–4
   technology 39
Press Complaints Commission 96
primary research 4–5, 85, 108–10
print production
   grading criteria 106, 122, 142, 192
   investigation of 111, 113
   learning outcomes 118
   production process 158–63
   types of product 159–60
   ways of printing 158–9
   writing for 160–1
producers 64
production documentation 44–9
production logs 204–5
production process
   assessment criteria 142
   assignment tips 170
   audio production 151–7
   digital media 162–6
   grading criteria 142, 215

   grading tips 167
   health and safety 146–9
   learning outcomes 168
   optional units 142, 215
   personal, learning and thinking skills (PLTS) 149, 167
   print production 158–63
   reviewing 194–200
   risk assessments 147–9
   roles and responsibilities 144–6
   video production 150–1
   see also post-production; pre-production; reviews
production schedules 157
production software 39
products, media
   assessment criteria 78
   assignment tips 104
   audience responses to 98–102
   codes and conventions 92–3
   composition of 89–90
   constraints on 93–7
   construction of for specific audiences 88–97
   functional skills 84, 87, 97
   grading criteria 78
   grading tips 87, 97, 102
   identifying audiences for 80–7
   modes of addressing audiences 90–1
   personal, learning and thinking skills (PLTS) 84, 97
   research into audiences 85–7
   selection of material for 88
   types of print products 159–60
professional working practices 65–6
profile 80, 83
progressive web standards 166
proofreading 49
proposals 126, 135
prototypes 163
psychographics 82
public relations 64
publicity 64
punctuality 72

Q

qualifications 70–1
quantitative and qualitative information 6–8

R

race discrimination 93
radio production
   links and idents 182–3
   post-production 181–3
   see also audio production
reading a text 99
recce 127
recording/editing formats 151
reflective learners 36, 43, 207
regulatory bodies 95
reliability 72

rendering 180
reports 115
research
assessment criteria 2
assignment tips 26
into audiences 85–7
choosing media product for 12
comparison of similar products 16
functional skills 5, 17, 19, 24
grading criteria 2
grading tips 11, 19
for a media production 18–19
personal, learning and thinking skills
(PLTS) 5, 17, 19, 24
during pre-production 127–8
presenting results of 20–4
primary 4–5, 85, 108–10
production processes 16
purpose of 13
quantitative and qualitative
information 6–8
record of 9–10
secondary 6, 111
target audience, classification of
13–15
techniques 8–9
reviews
assessment criteria 192
assignment tips 210
feedback on products 205–6
of finished product 201–4
grading criteria 192, 216
grading tips 207
information sources for 204–6
learning outcomes 208
optional units 192, 216
production logs 204–5
production process 194–200
suitability of product for audience 200
team contributions 198–200
of technical/creative competence
196–7
time management 195–6

using new media formats 206
risk assessments 127, 147–9
roles and responsibilities 144–6
running order 181

S
salaries in the creative media sector 69
sales and marketing 63, 64
secondary research 6, 85, 111
self appraisal 73
self-managers 167, 188
set designers 64
sexual orientation 83
size of organizations 59–60
skills and qualifications 70–1
social class of audience 15
sound effects 155
sources of graphics and images 163
station managers 64
storyboards 46
structure of media sector. see creative
media sector
SWOT analysis 126–7

T
target audience, classification of 13–15
team workers 5, 84
teams, reviewing contributions 198–200
technical directors 64
technical producers 64
technical skills 62, 63, 64
technology for presentations 39
television genres 92
test screenings 205
test shoots and recordings 130
testing 165
3D computer game engines
grading criteria 122, 142, 213
learning outcomes 118
time management 195–6
timeline 180
titles 180
transferable skills 72

transitions 39, 180
treatments 44
trimming 180
2D computer game engines
grading criteria 122, 142, 213
learning outcomes 118
2D digital art for computer games
grading criteria 106, 122, 216
learning outcomes 118

U
usability standards 166

V
video production
continuity 151
grading criteria 122, 142, 172, 192
paperwork 150
post-production 174–80
production process 150–1
visual aids 39
vocabulary 47–8
voice 32–3, 42

W
wages in the creative media sector 69
web authoring
grading criteria 106, 122, 142, 192
learning outcomes 118
web designers 64
web developers 64
wipes 180
working hours limits 67
working practices 65–6
writers 64
writing for the creative media
grading criteria 213, 214, 215, 216
investigation of 114
learning outcomes 118
print production 160–1
written communication 44–9